101
SUPPORT
GROUP
ACTIVITIES

for
Teenagers
at Risk
for Chemical
Dependence
or
Related
Problems

Martin Fleming

JOHNSON INSTITUTE

HAZELDEN®

Hazelden
15251 Pleasant Valley Road
Center City, MN 55012
1-800-328-9000
http://www.hazelden.org

Library of Congress Cataloging-in-Publication Data

Fleming, Martin.
    101 support group activities for teenagers at risk for chemical dependence or related problems:
a leader's manual for secondary educators and other professionals / Martin Fleming.
      p. cm.
    Includes bibliographical references.
    ISBN 1-56246-042-0
    1. Teenagers–United States–Alcohol use. 2. Teenagers–United States–Drug use. 3. Alcoholism–United States–Prevention. 4. Drug Abuse–United States–Prevention. 5. Group relations training. 6. Self-help groups–United States–Activity programs. 7. Counseling in secondary education–United States. I. Title. II. Title: One hundred one support group activities for teenagers at risk for chemical dependence or related problems.
HV5135.F538 1992
362.29'18'0835–dc20

92-18786
CIP

PRINTED IN THE UNITED STATES OF AMERICA
    5 4 3

Acknowledgments

First off, there's Lenore Franzen, my editor who's able to turn carbon into diamonds (though the process isn't as painful as the parallel might suggest), I'd also like to thank Willard Lubka for his helpful input and, in particular, three other support group leaders for the activities they shared with me: Shelley Hansen, Jenni Spear, Marilyn North.

Dedication

To my parents

Table of Contents

Introduction

This book is a collection of activities I've accumulated over the years from leading support groups for young people experiencing troubles because of their alcohol and other drug use. Some activities are well-worn favorites I've used in hundreds of support groups; others are reserved for special occasions or unusual situations. Regardless, all the activities are structured with three main goals in mind: helping these young people see the problems they're having with alcohol and other drugs, encouraging them to look at personal issues that underlie their chemical use, and assisting them in making the necessary changes based on what they learned in the support group. This three-step process—breaking through denial, creating insight, encouraging behavioral change—serves as a springboard that will help these young people get back to the awesome adventure of growing up.

THE CHALLENGE OF ADOLESCENCE

Adolescence is that turbulent chapter in life after childhood and before adulthood. For our purposes (and the target of this book's activities) this encompasses students from grade 7 through grade 12. This period of transition is filled with challenges. Young people want to be able to take care of themselves and be "grown up." There's an intense, all-powerful need to be accepted by their peers at whatever cost. There's pressure to decide what you want to "be" as an adult. And let's not forget all those new hormones surging through their bloodstreams.

It's no surprise, really, that so many of today's youth use chemicals. Most adolescents mistakenly believe that using alcohol or other drugs will turn you into an adult; they also discover that it's a quick way to be popular and accepted, and, especially important, that chemicals make you feel good, at least for awhile.

But, as is often the case in life, the shortcut has some hidden costs. Many life skills are learned during adolescence: dealing with feelings, being responsible, setting and working towards goals, problem solving, handling independence, to name a few. If a young person deals with her anger by going to a keg party and getting drunk, she is missing out on an important lesson that may handicap her in the future. If an awkward-feeling young man can't interact with young women unless he's smoked a few joints, you can be sure he will continue to turn to this solution in the future.

IT'S NOT BLACK AND WHITE

There are different degrees of what people often refer to as "having a problem" with alcohol or other drugs. Some young people misuse or abuse chemicals; it's possible for them to learn different ways of, say, dealing with their feelings or coping with peer pressure. They can let go of the chemicals and get on with the tasks of adolescence. Unfortunately, there are other young people whose relationship with chemicals has become primary. When this relationship becomes more important than anything else, it is called chemical dependence. The exact causes of chemical dependence aren't well understood yet, but many factors are clear: repeated use, emotional problems, societal influences, and genetic predisposition.

It's much more difficult for these young people to give up the chemicals and move on. They are stuck. Usually it takes an intensive therapeutic experience, such as a chemical dependence treatment center, to jerk them out of the rut and teach them how to stay clean and sober from alcohol and other drugs.

In a typical support group you'll see different levels of alcohol and other drug problems, so you can expect different goals and outcomes. One student in the group might have been at a party that was busted. She drinks only occasionally and this is her first time in trouble because of it. For her, the support group is an opportunity to understand the possible future consequences of continued use, and to learn new ways to interact with her friends that don't involve drinking.

Most likely, a few students in the group will have already developed a moderate problem. These group members will be more difficult to reach because they'll be protective of their relationship with their chemicals. What's the plan of attack? These students first need to see the reality of how the chemicals are messing things up for them by breaking through their denial. Then you must teach them different, effective ways of dealing with their feelings, responding to stress, and connecting with their peers. And, since their connection with alcohol and other drugs has an established track record, you'll also need to expose them to refusal skills (how to say no assertively) and natural highs (how to have fun without chemicals), or else they will fall back into the rut of what's convenient and predictable.

Finally, you will encounter students who are truly chemically dependent. They've turned defenses into an art form. A support group usually won't get these adolescents clean and sober. The tools a support group offers just aren't powerful enough to accomplish this task. But a support group is still crucial for these students because it's the first step in creating an awareness painful enough to motivate them to move into another program that is powerful enough to help them, typically a treatment center. The support group experience also allows both the student and caregivers to collect data that will help them determine the true extent of the problem. This information can then be used to stage a successful intervention, a process of presenting reality to the student in a manner he or she can hear.*

WHO THIS BOOK IS FOR

This book is primarily a tool for experienced support group leaders who are looking for new and better ways of reaching young people affected by chemical dependence. Though it is written with schools in mind, the activities can be readily adapted to a variety of settings: aftercare programs, therapy sessions, treatment center, youth group. If you are a beginning support group leader and have more questions than answers at this point, I suggest you read my book **Conducting Support Groups for Students Affected by Chemical Dependence**. This is the basic text for learning how to lead support groups and how to integrate them into your school. Being a support group leader can be a challenge and it requires some training and background in chemical dependence. This book of activities won't teach you how to run a support group—it assumes you already know. Think of this as a cookbook. It doesn't teach you how to cook, but it provides a wealth of new recipes to try.

THE STRUCTURE OF THIS BOOK

The activities in this book are divided into 10 categories:
Group development activities help a collection of nervous, hostile, and uncomfortable students become a cohesive and productive group.
Self-exploration activities help group members understand who they are, what they want, and what they need to change.
Family relations activities help group members understand the emotional dynamics in

---

*A thorough discussion of the process of intervention is beyond the scope of this book. *Choice and Consequences* by Dick Schaefer provides much more information on this topic (see Resources).

their family and what they can do to make things better for themselves.

Chemical dependence information activities help students understand the dynamics of the disease and how it may be affecting them.

Self-assessment activities encourage group members to take an honest look at their personal relationship with alcohol and other drugs.

Getting additional help activities introduce group members to community resources they can turn to for further help and support.

Goals and decisions activities provide motivation and tools for action based on the insights students gained in the group.

Peer pressure activities help group members learn how to deal with peer pressure in constructive ways.

Stress-reduction activities teach group members how to recognize and manage their stress.

Group Challenge activities empower group members to work together as a team.

The techniques for teaching these concepts are as varied as the activities. Some activities are discussion-based while others incorporate a game. Since many students can express themselves readily through art, many activities challenge students to draw their thoughts and feelings. And there are also some activities that use physical motion and noncompetitive games as an avenue for personal growth.

Though the heart of this book is the collection of activities, a brief description of a support group in action is provided in chapter 1, curriculum development is outlined in chapter 2, and additional resources are listed in the final section.

Each activity is organized in a similar fashion. Goals are outlined at the top of the page, followed by a brief description of the activity. This will help when you're looking for a particular kind of group activity and don't want to have to read several pages just to find out what the activity entails.

Once you've found an activity you're interested in using, the second half of the page provides detailed directions, a materials list, worksheets (which have a "Look" icon on them) for you to photocopy and distribute in group, and examples of artwork when necessary for clarification. It's assumed that students will have a pencil or pen and that there is a blackboard or marker board in the room. When specific information is required for an activity, there is a **For Your Information** section included so you won't have to go out and hunt down additional resources to present the activity. Except where noted, all the activities are designed to fit within the time constraints of a typical school class period, say 50 minutes.

THE RATINGS BOX

Stage:	1-4
Challenge:	LOW
Grades:	ALL

You might have already noticed that accompanying each activity is a selection code heading with the categories **Stage, Challenge,** and **Grades.** Starting at the bottom, Grades refers to the academic grades the particular activity is designed for. Note that the term "all" refers to 7 to 12, not grades 1 to 12.

Challenge describes the degree of intimacy, honesty, or confrontation inherent to the activity. Activities designated as low challenge are ideal for beginning groups. Moderately challenging activities will help a support group begin to take the risks necessary to achieve intimacy. Activities with a high level of challenge are often saved for a group that has spent considerable time together. This isn't always the case, though. Sometimes support group leaders, because they have only a few weeks available for the group to meet or because they want to get right to the heart of the matter, will use a high-challenge activity in the beginning stages of the group. **My Chemical Story** (activity # 66) is an example of a high-challenge activity you may wish to use as early as the second session because of the intimacy it helps create.

Stage refers to the developmental stage for which the specific activity is appropriate. The coding system uses the numbers 1 through 4. The first stage is one of building trust and getting acquainted. Group members need to become comfortable with each other and understand how their group will function concerning rules, goals, and expectations.

In stage 2, the newness is over and now group members need to begin working together. There will be conflict, struggles to define roles, as well as testing of limits and your authority. It's like buying a car: first you look it over; then you kick the tires and take it for a spin.

Once the group has moved through stage 2, then it can get on with the real work of a support group. In stage 3, group members are comfortable and trusting of each other. It's in this setting that students can really begin to take risks and talk about what's going on in their personal lives.

And because all support group must come to an end, stage 4 describes the process of closure that a group experiences. This should involve more than simply saying "good bye." Stage 4 is a time for students to reflect on what they've learned and experienced as well as clarify what they will do differently in the future.

Having described these four stages, I feel I should point out that a group for students in trouble with chemicals doesn't always progress through each stage. Sometimes the students' defensiveness and personal dysfunction keeps them from opening up and taking risks in the group. That's quite all right when it happens; many groups of this sort focus exclusively on self-assessment and reducing denial. A chemically dependent adolescent won't be able to deal with his feelings successfully as long as he continues to use chemicals. In this case, the goals of the group are breaking denial and helping to pave the way for a more intensive program, such as a treatment center. This isn't to say that these groups don't ever discuss feelings or resolve personal issues—just don't feel like the group (or you) failed if this doesn't take place.

When you refer to the selection code, bear in mind that these are only guidelines for choosing activities for your support group. An activity listed as being appropriate for older students might work very well with a group of younger but mature students, and a stage 3 activity could be modified for use with a fairly new support group.

Above all, as you use these new activities in group, remember that they are simply a medium, a tool, for teaching a concept or creating an opportunity for personal growth. What's really important is our young people and their struggles with the effects of chemical dependence. But, even so, we can't just wave a magic wand or simply tell them not to worry. We must point them down the right path, assisting them in developing their own ideas and insights. So, in this light, the tools are important. A house to keep you safe and warm might be the goal, but it must be made, step by step. And these activities are the tools you can use to help students take those steps from despair to hope, from insight to action.

Chapter One:
For the Beginning Support
Group Leader

Let's look in the window of a support group at work. Students are sitting in a tight circle of comfortable chairs, talking about things important and personal. The co-leaders are sitting across from each other, guiding the process as well as participating in the discussion.

The session starts out with a brief warm-up activity to get students focused on their feelings. Then one of the leaders introduces the session topic. After a brief discussion, the students are given a worksheet that helps them describe their own personal history with various mind-altering chemicals. Once everyone has finished, the group leader brings them back together and asks for a volunteer to begin the discussion. A young man named Tom with long hair hanging down over most of his face nervously begins to rattle off his own history of chemical use: "I started drinking liquor that I stole from my Dad when I was 11. I smoked my first joint the summer of seventh grade. By the time I was 14 I was getting high most every day."

When he's finished, one of the group leaders asks him what has changed about his chemical use from a few years back to now. Tom shrugs his shoulders.

"What do the rest of you think about Tom's use of chemicals?" the leader asks the rest of the group.

"Well," says a girl who's Tom's friend, "Tom used to only do it a little—you know, now and then—but now he's stoned all the time."

The leader looks at Tom. "Is that true?"

"I guess so," Tom mumbles, looking down at the floor.

"Are you concerned about that?" The group leader won't let it go.

"Maybe."

"Maybe?"

"Well, yeah, like if I can't graduate next year."

The group leader pauses for a moment to think. "Will you graduate if you come to class high all the time?"

"No."

"So, are you concerned about your pot smoking?"

Tom grunts.

"What's that?"

"Okay, yes," Tom says, annoyed.

"Yes, what?"

"Yes, I'm concerned about my pot smoking!"

When he is finished another student begins, and then another. A few minutes before the session is over, one of the co-leaders collects the worksheets and they spend the last minutes talking about what they learned.

Of course, this is merely an example. Support groups change from week to week. And support group leaders have differing styles of running group, too. Controlling or loose, intellectual or with their hearts on their sleeves, confrontational or laid back, the flavor of the group depends on the personality of the leaders as well as the students in the group.

We can control some variables of the group experience, such as the physical qualities of the group room, the number of students in group, and the frequency of the group meetings. Every support group leader must make these decisions based on his or her own particular situation. Fortunately, collective experience has brought us practical solutions. Here are some typical questions asked by beginning support group leaders and the answers that work in most situations:

HOW MANY STUDENTS SHOULD I HAVE IN MY GROUP?

The maximum number is much more critical than the minimum number. Six to eight students is a good size; ten should be your upper limit. Groups larger than this can have a purpose—a large keg party being busted resulting in many referrals to the group, for example—but, it's best to think of this size as a class experience—focusing more on information and less on creating emotional intimacy—rather than a group experience.

IS IT OKAY TO MIX STUDENTS IN A GROUP?

You'll find it helpful to keep the grades separate. Ninth graders, for example, are quite different from seventh grade students in their interaction styles, maturity, as well as degree of involvement with chemicals. Mixing genders usually isn't a problem. In fact, it can be beneficial. Balance is important, though. The dynamics can get uncomfortable if, for example, there is only one girl in a group of boys.

There is another important dynamic to be aware of concerning the mix of students. Don't mix a number of harmfully involved students with one or two students who are only beginning to have a problem with chemicals. The group can have a negative outcome for these two students on the fringe because they might begin to idolize and imitate the other, more troubled students.

Fortunately, the reverse can be used to your advantage. One or two chemically dependent students in a group where the majority aren't as harmfully involved tend to feel very uneasy because their chemical use and consequences are painfully evident.

HOW OFTEN SHOULD A SUPPORT GROUP MEET?

Typically, groups meet once a week.

SHOULD GROUPS MEET DURING THE SAME PERIOD EACH SESSION?

While meeting the same period has its advantages—easy for the students to remember, easy for the leaders to prepare—it means that students miss the same class week after week. The best solution is to rotate the group time each week: second period one week, third period next week, and so on.

HOW MANY SESSIONS SHOULD THERE BE?

It depends on the nature of the group. Groups that focus mostly on self-assessment tend to run 6 to 10 weeks. Groups that also focus on underlying emotional issues of the members are longer, often 8 to 14 weeks.

SHOULD MY GROUP MEET DURING OR AFTER SCHOOL?

Most of these types of group meet during school, although some schools schedule the group after school. This second strategy is typically used when all of the members are participating in the group because of consequences, such as being caught getting high at a school dance or with alcohol in a locker.

WHERE IS A GOOD PLACE TO HOLD GROUP?

The ideal group room is small, carpeted, and equipped with comfortable chairs. It's also nice to have pillows for when the group is on the floor. There shouldn't be any windows, and the room should be located in a quiet, low-traffic area. Of course, this is the ideal room, and many group leaders must settle for less. Whatever the room, it's important that it be the same room each session of group. Your last choice should be a standard classroom because of the hard floor, large size, chairs with built-in desks, and impersonal atmosphere.

WHAT SHOULD I CALL MY GROUP?

Common names are Drug Information Group, Awareness Group, or Insight Group.

WHAT RULES SHOULD I MAKE FOR MY GROUP?

The fewer the better. Typically rules cover confidentiality, chemical use or possession (No chemicals in you or on you!), and regular attendance. "Everybody must talk about their feelings" is a hope or expectation—don't make it a rule. And don't make rules that you aren't going to enforce consistently. Students get enough of this inconsistency at home. Make your rules specific, reasonable, and enforceable.

SHOULD I HAVE A CO-LEADER IN MY GROUP?

In a word, yes. Sometimes conditions make it necessary to run group solo, but whenever possible have a helper. Co-leaders can come to the rescue when the group gets unmanageable or when you're not picking up on something that a student is feeling. Beginning group leaders should always have the assistance of a seasoned pro.

WHERE DO I DRAW THE LINE WITH GROUP CONFIDENTIALITY?

Generally speaking, anything that a student says in group stays in group. But, in situations of abuse (physical or sexual), harming one's self (suicide) or harming others (assault or homicide), you must report this information. These exceptions to the confidentiality rule should be explained during the first session of group.

On the other hand, your impression of a student and any concerns you have about his or her chemical use can, and should, be shared in situations where it will be constructive, such as a meeting between parents and school to determine whether a referral should be made for a chemical dependence assessment.

SHOULD I ASK STUDENTS TO SIGN NO-USE CONTRACTS?

It depends on how the contract is presented and what the consequences are. Often, when you demand students to sign a no-use contract, the group becomes dishonest because when a member does use and breaks his contract (which will happen with some), he won't talk about it.

You may wish to make the no-use contract optional. This way, students who elect to make this commitment, and then fail, can't say, "Well, I didn't have any intention of staying clean anyway." Instead, the reality is they wanted to abstain for the duration of the contract but were unable to. This information pierces through their denial.

Some students will enter this group already on a no-use contract between them and their parents, the courts, and school. Of course, your support group will then be an extension of this preexisting contract.

IS IT ALL RIGHT FOR STUDENTS TO BE PRESSURED TO ATTEND THIS GROUP EVEN THOUGH THEY DON'T WANT TO BE THERE?

Yes. Even though students in this category might not be honest about their chemical use at first, group process—the slow building of trust and intimacy amongst group members—will warm up even the most closed of students. Besides, even if they don't say a word, they still have ears to hear with.

WHAT'S THE NEXT STEP FOR STUDENTS AFTER THEY'VE FINISHED THE GROUP?

This depends on what brought them to the group in the first place. Students participating because of consequences should be involved in an exit conference with representatives from the school, parents, support group leader, and other involved caregivers. This meeting can be used to decide what would be the most constructive next step for this student, such as a no-use contract, assessment, referral to a treatment center, or family therapy.

Some students who volunteered to be in group will have made a decision to abstain from alcohol and other drugs but will need help honoring this commitment. They may wish to join a different support group, or spend individual time with a school counselor.

And then there are some group members who got what they needed from the group and whose personal circumstances don't warrant further attention on your part.

The above merely touches on some rather complex and thorny issues surrounding the reality of support groups in a school setting. Again, if you are contemplating initiating a support group in your school, you need more information and training. *Conducting Support Groups For Students Affected by Chemical Dependence* will assist you in developing the framework necessary for support groups to function effectively.

Chapter Two:
Designing A Curriculum

With a skilled leader, a single group session has a carefully orchestrated flow from beginning to end. And in the bigger picture, so, too, does an entire group curriculum. Rather than being put together in a random fashion, group activities should be in a specific sequence that encourages learning and growth. This chapter outlines the five key steps for designing your own group curriculum.

STEP 1

Your first task as a group leader is to decide on the total number of sessions your group will meet. Most Drug Information Groups have a total of six to twelve sessions. If your group meets weekly, then this fits comfortably into an average school quarter, while leaving time to meet with students referred to group at the beginning of the quarter and not interfere with quarterly tests.

STEP 2

Once you decide how many times your group will meet, it's tempting to begin planning what you'll do during those sessions.

Stop right there! **First select your group goals**. Just as the carpenter draws up the house plan and then makes a list of tools she'll need to build this house, make a list of the goals you would like to meet in your support group. Don't be concerned yet with a specific order. Example 2.1 will help get you started with your own list.

STEP 3

Most likely, you will have listed more goals than can be realistically addressed in the time constraints of a typical support group. You'll need to prioritize. (I've found that the least painful way to whittle down this list is to begin crossing out the least important goals first.) How many goals can you realistically try to address in your support group? As a general guideline, you shouldn't have more goals than you do sessions of group. Actually, since virtually every support group's initial session is used to discuss the rules of the group and reduce students' uneasiness and the final session is set aside for closure, your number of goals should be the total number of sessions minus two. Which goals are the most important to address in a support group? Here are the basic categories of goals that are common to nearly all Drug Information Group curricula:

Education - teach students about chemical dependence.

Self-assessment - encourage students to take an honest look at their chemical use.

Feelings - help students learn how to recognize, understand, express, and cope with their feelings.

Self-worth - help students feel better about themselves, assert their personal power and autonomy, and feel validated.

Coping - teach problem-solving skills and offer practical solutions.

Refusal skills - offer students practical tools for staying abstinent.

STEP 4

Once you have made a grocery list of goals, it's time to begin shopping for activities. This is the fun part. Page through the sections in this book and select activities that both meet your identified goals and are appropriate for the students in your group. You should choose one activity for each goal on your list. Don't be afraid to try new activities—you might be pleasantly surprised.

STEP 5

Now that you have a goal and a corresponding activity for each session of group, it's time to place these activities in a sequence that's most helpful to the group members. Generally speaking, the initial sessions should be used to calm nerves and reduce tension. The middle sessions are the meat of the group, introducing new concepts, breaking down resistance, and promoting self-awareness. The final sessions of group recap learning and facilitate closure. Example 2.2 is a worksheet that will guide you through all five steps of the planning process.

For those of you who, at this point, would rather stick with a curriculum that has been field-tested and proven to work well, I've included two options in Example 2.3. Feel free to follow these exactly or modify them to meet your specific needs. The Resources section also lists several sources of group curricula.

Example 2.1: Group Goals

- Teach students the dynamics of chemical use, abuse, and dependence.
- Teach students the disease concept of chemical dependence.
- Help students feel better about themselves.
- Encourage students to abstain from alcohol and other drugs.
- Help students identify, understand, and express their feelings.
- Build self-confidence and self-esteem.
- Confront students' denial.
- Inform students of their high risk for becoming chemically dependent.
- Help students learn how to have fun without chemicals.
- Teach stress-management techniques.
- Provide opportunities for students to help their peers.
- Motivate students to seek treatment.
- Create a safe place to talk about feelings.
- Offer the students stable relationships with adults.
- Help students identify their emotional needs.
- Help students improve their relationships with family members.
- Strengthen coping skills.
- Teach healthy decision-making skills.
- Help them find ways to deal with their painful feelings.
- Develop competency with age-appropriate tasks.
- Improve academic performance.
- Make an assessment of students' chemical use.
- Help school staff gain insight into a student's problems.
- Encourage students to use community support resources.
- Help students begin to trust others.
- Encourage intimacy and bonding within the support group.
- Facilitate termination of the group experience.

Example 2.2: Curriculum Planning Worksheet

STEP 1:

How many sessions will your group have?_____

STEP 2:

Make a list of goals for your group:

STEP 3:

Select one goal for each session except the first and last.

continued on next page

STEP 4:

Select a group activity for each goal.

Goal	Activity
_____	_____
_____	_____
_____	_____
_____	_____
_____	_____
_____	_____
_____	_____
_____	_____
_____	_____
_____	_____
_____	_____
_____	_____
_____	_____
_____	_____

STEP 5:

Organize the goals and the corresponding activities in a constructive sequence:

Session #	Goal	Activity
_____	_____	_____
_____	_____	_____
_____	_____	_____
_____	_____	_____
_____	_____	_____
_____	_____	_____
_____	_____	_____
_____	_____	_____
_____	_____	_____
_____	_____	_____
_____	_____	_____
_____	_____	_____

Example 2.3:
Curriculum Examples

EXAMPLE A: This is a straightforward curriculum that will work well in most situations. It has simple goals—education, self-assessment, and looking at family issues—and is short enough so you can run two group cycles in one academic quarter. All of this being the case, it might be your first choice for an introductory group that fits the requirements of a school policy referring all students suspected of chemical use to an in-school support group.

SESSION 1

INTRODUCTIONS
Goals: Establish group rapport
            Explain group rules and goals
Activity: Interview Exercise (activity #3)

SESSION 2

HISTORY OF STUDENTS' CHEMICAL USE
Goal: Identify history of chemical use
Activity: My Chemical History (activity #57)

SESSION 3

REASONS FOR USING CHEMICALS
Goal: Identify relationship between feelings and chemical use
Activity: Chemicals and Feelings (activity #61)

SESSION 4

DEFENSES
Goal: Identify defenses related to chemical use
Activity: Chemicals and Defenses (activity #62)

SESSION 5

CONSEQUENCES
Goal: Identify consequences related to chemical use
Activity: My Chemical Story (activity #66)

SESSION 6

CHEMICAL DEPENDENCE IN THE FAMILY
Goals: Identify students affected by familial chemical dependence
            Help affected students understand they are at high risk for becoming chemically dependent
Activity: Is There Chemical Dependence in My Family? (activity #38)

SESSION 7

CLOSURE
Goals: Final personal assessment
            Develop plans and goals
Activity: The Last Word (activity #85)

EXAMPLE B:

This curriculum is designed for students who are considered high risk but who aren't using chemicals yet or, if so, are only experimenting. The activities focus on teaching group members healthy living skills—dealing with feelings, handling stress, refusal skills—that then reduce the chances that they will develop a damaging relationship with alcohol and other drugs.

SESSION 1

INTRODUCTIONS
Goals: Establish group rapport
          Explain group rules and goals
Activity: Two Coyotes and a Rabbit (activity #12)

SESSION 2

FEELINGS AWARENESS
Goal: Establish connection between feelings and behavior
Activity: Five Familiar Feelings (activity #24)

SESSION 3

FEELINGS AWARENESS, CONT.
Goal: Teach students how to cope with their feelings
Activity: What Should I Do with My Feelings? (activity #25)

SESSION 4

FAMILY RELATIONSHIPS
Goal: Explore family dynamics
Activity: Family Collage (activity #36)

SESSION 5

CHEMICALS AND BEHAVIOR
Goal: Help students understand why they use chemicals
Activity: Why Do People Use Chemicals? (activity #40)

SESSION 6

DECISION-MAKING SKILLS
Goal: Learn effective decision-making skills
Activity: Making Choices (activity #77)

SESSION 7

REFUSAL SKILLS
Goal: Learn how to resist peer pressure
Activity: Learning How to Say "No" (activity 89)

SESSION 8

COPING WITH STRESS
Goal: Identify helpful coping strategies
Activity: My Coping Style (activity #90)

SESSION 9

GROUP CHALLENGE
Goal: Reinforce chemical dependence concepts
Activity: The Chemical Dependence Adventure Game (activity #100)

SESSION 10

CLOSURE
Goals: Encourage goal-setting
          Support personal changes made by group members
Activity: From Now On (activity #81)

The Activities

Section A:
Group Development Activities

The activities in this first section will transform somewhat hostile students sitting nervously in a circle of chairs into a relaxed and productive support group. A tall order? Not really. Actually, you'll find that after getting the young people to come to the initial group session you're already halfway there. Remember, many of these students are a mess—both inside and outside—and they want to talk about their pain, lessen their burdens, get some answers.

But most of these students don't know how to talk about their problems or work together as a team, let alone how a support group functions. They are used to going it alone with their feelings and struggles. Isolation, staying numb with chemicals, and an elaborate defense system have protected them so far, but support groups encourage just the opposite. Though the focus isn't specifically chemical dependence, all of the activities in this first section are important because they build a secure foundation upon which more challenging activities can be presented. Breaking the ice, building themes of commonality, encouraging students to support each other, and providing transitions to and from the "real world" outside of group are all bricks carefully laid for the structure yet to come.

1
Warm-ups

GOALS: ▶
- Provide a transition from a cognitive to an affective learning mode
- Help students focus on group process
- Energize a lethargic group

DESCRIPTION: ▶

Warm-ups are various, brief activities used during the first few minutes of group to help students focus on their feelings and group process.

DIRECTIONS: ▶

When first introducing this activity, you should select the warm-up question, but in the future appoint a different group member to be responsible for the warm-up question for each session. That person may either make up a question or choose one from the list you provide (see following page). This activity isn't the mainstay of a group session; it's simply a way to become focused on group process—not unlike a runner stretching before a workout. Five minutes is a good time guideline for this activity.

NOTES: ▶

In order to place more responsibility on the group, you could ask the student in charge of the Warm-up for the current session to assign next session's Warm-up to another group member. This process can then continue each session of group.

MATERIALS: ▶

Warm-up question list.

Warm-up Questions

- Name a simple and a difficult emotion for you to talk about.

- Are you more like your mother or your father? Why?

- Communicate nonverbally how you are feeling.

- When somebody hurts your feelings, what do you do?

- What do you do when you are angry?

- Tell the group one thing that you appreciate about yourself.

- After everyone is sitting in a tight circle, have them turn to their right and massage the neck of their neighbor.

- If you were an animal, what type would you be? Why?

- Demonstrate your personality when you were a little child.

- Name one physical quality about you that you like.

- Identify one quality that you have to offer a friend.

- When was the last time you cried? What were the tears about?

- When you really need to talk to somebody, whom do you turn to?

- What is one thing that people don't understand about you?

- When you need alone time, where do you go and what do you do?

2
Cool-downs

GOALS: ▶
- Provide closure for group activities
- Clarify learning

DESCRIPTION: ▶ Cool-downs are brief activities that bring a raw or unfinished group session to closure and reinforce learning.

DIRECTIONS: ▶ Reserve the last five minutes or so of each group session for this activity. Choose an option from the following page, appropriate to the activity the group has just finished, and ask group members to respond.

NOTES: ▶ When a group session hasn't been very intense, you probably won't need a closing activity. You may wish to leave it up to the group to decide. You could also ask group members to choose the closing question.

MATERIALS: ▶ List of **Cool-downs**.

Cool-downs List

- Ask group members what they learned about themselves today.

- Tell a joke.

- Ask everyone to get up and stretch.

- Hold hands and be silent for three minutes.

- Tell the group members something you appreciate about them.

- Ask a member of the group to summarize what happened during the group.

- Ask group members to tell a person in group who is having an especially difficult time something they appreciate about her.

- Ask group members what they need from the rest of the group.

- Ask the group what they would like to do next week.

- Ask group members if they have anything they would like to say to the rest of the group.

3
Interview Exercise

GOALS: ▶
- Establish group rapport
- Ease tension in a beginning group

DESCRIPTION: ▶ Group members interview each other and then introduce their partner to the rest of the group.

DIRECTIONS: ▶ Pair members of the group together—preferably with someone they don't know very well—and instruct them to ask each other the questions on the worksheet you've handed out (see following page). Position these diads around the group room so that they have a little privacy. The interviewer should write his partner's answers on his own sheet next to the questions. When the interviewer is finished asking questions, the pair should reverse roles. After everybody has finished, bring them back into a circle and ask each person to introduce his or her partner to the group and share the recorded responses.

NOTES: ▶ Depending on the time remaining in the session, ask follow-up questions to the students' answers—"Oh, so you like rock climbing. Where do you go to do that?" for example. This will both encourage discussion as well as help group members to feel valued and important.

MATERIALS: ▶ **Interview Exercise** worksheet.

Interview

INSTRUCTIONS: Ask your partner these questions and write their answers next to the questions on your sheet.

1. What is your name?

2. Where were you born?

3. What do you like to do in your spare time?

4. What is something that really bugs you?

5. If you had five thousand dollars, what would you do with it?

6. What is your favorite music group?

7. What one word would best describe you?

8. What are you looking forward to this year?

9. What aren't you looking forward to this year?

10. What are you afraid of?

Now, think of two additional questions to ask your partner:

11. Question:

   Answer:

12. Question:

   Answer:

4
Why Am I Here?

GOALS: ▶
- Encourage self-disclosure
- Reduce hostility
- Provide a foundation for future group activities

DESCRIPTION: ▶

Group members explain the circumstances that have brought them to the group.

DIRECTIONS: ▶

Ask group members to share in some detail why it is that they are participating in this support group. During this initial session, many group members will be somewhat hostile and defiant. That's okay. Encourage them to be honest with their thoughts and feelings about being in the group. Encourage them to blow off some steam—after all, it's not your fault that they're in this group! If they are in the group because of consequences, make sure that they explain this to the group. "I was caught with vodka in my locker last week and they told me that I either had to come to this group or be suspended for ten days," for example. Here are additional questions to consider:

QUESTIONS: ▶
- How do you feel about being here?
- What happened that got you here?
- Are there other consequences besides being in this group?
- How does your parent(s) feel about what has happened?
- Do you think you should be here?
- Do you have to be here? What happens if you don't come?

MATERIALS: ▶

None required.

5
Take What You Need

GOALS: ▶
- Encourage self-disclosure
- Reduce communication barriers

DESCRIPTION: ▶ Group members volunteer information about themselves in whatever areas they choose.

DIRECTIONS: ▶ Place a container of M&Ms or a roll of toilet paper in the center of the group circle. Tell group members to take what they need. At this point, don't give any further instructions. After everyone has taken what they want, tell the group that everyone must share one thing at a time about themselves for each M&M or sheet of toilet paper they have taken. Go around the circle as many times as are required. Group members should be encouraged to share anything they wish.

NOTES: ▶ If you use M&Ms, it would be a good idea to limit the amount you place in the circle. Otherwise some students could grab such a large handful that they would need several hours of sharing time!

MATERIALS: ▶ M&Ms or toilet paper.

6
Five Things We Have In Common

GOALS: ▶
- Establish group rapport
- Encourage honest communication

DESCRIPTION: ▶ Group members break into teams of two or three, and find five things that they all share in common.

DIRECTIONS: ▶ Depending on the number of students in the group, divide the students into teams of two or three. Instruct them to discover something that each member of the team shares in common. This could be age, owning a dog, or liking the same music. After the team has found this commonality, ask them to repeat the task, but this time give them a focus, such as characteristics of parents, things they're afraid of, something that really bugs them about their family, what they think about people with drinking problems, or feelings they don't like dealing with, for example. Each time you repeat the task, make the specific focus more difficult and personal.

NOTES: ▶ You may wish to shift team members at some point in this activity so that students have a chance to get to know other group members.

MATERIALS: ▶ None required.

7
Sentence Stems

GOALS: ▶
- Encourage honest communication
- Allow students to determine the session's focus

DESCRIPTION: ▶
Group members take turns choosing and completing sentence stems.

DIRECTIONS: ▶
Distribute copies of a list of questions (see following page) and ask each group member to choose and then answer a question in turn. After a student answers a question, the rest of the group can ask for more information or clarification. Tell the group they can make up their own questions if they can't find a question on the sheet that they like.

NOTES: ▶
Give everyone a copy of the questions, so time isn't wasted while students read through the list looking for a question to answer. A variation of this activity would be to ask the person who just answered a question to choose the question for the next group member.

MATERIALS: ▶
Sentence Stems handout for each group member.

Sentence Stems

1. Right now I'm feeling . . .

2. When I'm alone I feel . . .

3. When I'm surrounded by people I feel . . .

4. One thing that I hate is . . .

5. One thing that I really like about myself is . . .

6. When I'm feeling sad I . . .

7. The last time I cried was . . .

8. When I daydream it's usually about . . .

9. I'm afraid of . . .

10. I'm the happiest when . . .

11. One thing that really worries me is . . .

12. If I could change one thing about myself it would be . . .

13. If I could be with anyone right now I would be with . . .

14. The family member I'm closest to is . . .

15. If I was really honest with my father I would tell him . . .

16. One thing I regret about my life is . . .

17. If I only had one more day to live I would . . .

18. If I was really honest with my mother I would tell her . . .

19. One thing about me that nobody knows is . . .

20. I hope that someday in the future . . .

21. When I think about my family I feel . . .

22. Something I feel really embarrassed about is . . .

23. One thing about me I never want to change is . . .

24. One thing I feel really proud of is . . .

25. This support group has helped me to . . .

26. One thing I like about all of you is . . .

8
Spin the Bottle

Stage: 2-3

Challenge: HIGH

Grades: ALL

GOALS:

- Increase group awareness of chemical dependence consequences
- Encourage communication in group
- Gather information for group leaders

DESCRIPTION: ▶

Group members spin a bottle to select who is "it." This person draws from a stack of consequence cards and describes an instance when he experienced the consequence named on the card.

PROCEDURE: ▶

Make a number of 3 X 5 inch cards that have a consequence written on each one (see following page for a list of consequences). Place a pop bottle in the center of the circle. Have a student spin the bottle to start the game. Whomever the bottle points to must draw a card from the top of the deck and describe to the group when she has experienced that consequence, as well as explain the circumstances. If she hasn't experienced the consequence on the card, then she should draw another card.

After she's finished, she puts the card on the bottom of the deck and spins the bottle to determine who's next.

NOTES:

The right to pass should be respected during this activity.

MATERIALS:

Pop bottle, deck of consequence cards.

Consequences

- hung over

- arrested by the police for drug possession

- caught with alcohol or other drugs at school

- caught with alcohol or other drugs at home

- sent to a treatment center

- **have** gone in for an assessment

- kicked off an athletic team

- had a "bad trip"

- kicked out of school

- ran away from home

- attempted suicide

- **have** gotten a reputation as a "burn-out"

- got sick from bad drugs

- arrested for possession of alcohol (MIP)

- arrested for driving under the influence (DUI)

- went to juvenile court

- suspended from school

- been dropped by a girlfriend or boyfriend because of partying too much

- arrested by the police for selling drugs

- became addicted to alcohol or another drug
  referred to a school support group

- confronted by a teacher concerned about your chemical use

- parents called to school by principal to discuss your behavior

- flunked a class

- had a blackout

- had drug-using friends rip you off

9
Pulse

GOALS: ▶
- ■ Encourage group cooperation
- ■ Provide noncompetitive recreation

DESCRIPTION: ▶

One student stands in the center of the group circle while the remaining students join hands and pass a squeeze around the circle. The student in the center tries to locate this "pulse."

DIRECTIONS: ▶

Ask group members to form a tight circle sitting cross-legged and holding hands. Tell the group that the object of this game is to pass a "pulse" around the circle without getting caught. This pulse is represented by the squeezing of hands. When a group member feels her right hand getting squeezed, for example, she then passes the pulse on by squeezing the hand of the group member on her left. In this way the pulse is passed around the circle. The job of the person in the center is to catch the pulse after someone has received it, but before she has gotten rid of it.

Once the group has gotten the hang of passing the pulse, show them how they can reverse the direction of the pulse by squeezing back the same hand that squeezed theirs. This makes it much more difficult, but not impossible, for the person in the center to catch the pulse.

Once everyone is familiar with the game, start by asking someone to be in the center of the circle. Ask a student who is out of view of the person in the center to start the pulse. Once the pulse is moving, the student in the center is free to spin around and try to catch the pulse by pointing to someone and saying this person's name when he thinks she has the pulse. If he's correct, these two switch places and a new round starts; if he isn't correct, the game continues.

MATERIALS:

None required.

10
Grumpy

GOALS: ▶
- Provide noncompetitive recreation
- Break up the intensity of other group sessions

DESCRIPTION ▶

Group members try to make one designated person laugh.

DIRECTIONS: ▶

Explain to the group that this game involves trying hard to keep a straight face despite the antics performed by the rest of the group. Ask for a volunteer to be "it" first. She should sit in the center of the circle while the rest of the group tries their best to make her laugh or crack a smile, but without touching her in any way. Group members should take turns trying to evoke a laugh, working around the circle. Whoever is successful in making her laugh gets to be in the center next.

After playing this game for most of the group session, spend some time talking about laughter and its benefits. Ask the group to think about and then discuss in what situations they can let go and laugh.

MATERIALS: ▶

None required.

11
Responsi-ball

GOALS: ▶
- Encourage personal disclosure
- Create group intimacy

DESCRIPTION: ▶

Group members play a ball game that requires self-disclosure when the ball is dropped.

DIRECTIONS: ▶

With everyone sitting in a circle, explain to the group that they're to pass the ball back and forth in the circle without it touching the ground. They should hit the ball as in a game of volleyball—not throw it as if they were playing catch. When the ball hits the floor, the last two people to touch the ball—the one who hit it and the one to whom it was hit—must decide who's responsible for the ball falling to the floor. This person must then share something about herself with the group, such as what she likes to do in her spare time, who her favorite musician is, how many siblings she has. If the two can't decide who was responsible, then the group should choose (or you could ask both players to share something about themselves). The game continues in this fashion for the remainder of the session.

NOTES: ▶

The ball for this game should be very light, such as a foam rubber ball or even crumpled-up tissue paper with a plastic bag cover. Balloons rarely hit the ground, so little sharing takes place.

MATERIALS: ▶

Lightweight ball.

12
Two Coyotes and a Rabbit

GOALS: ▶
- Provide noncompetitive recreation
- Encourage students to talk about themselves

DESCRIPTION: ▶

Group members play a chase game using three balls and talk about themselves when they are caught.

DIRECTIONS: ▶

Ask group members to stand and form a circle. Throw two basketballs out into the circle and ask group members to begin passing them around. These two basketballs are the coyotes and they can only be passed to neighboring group members—not across the circle. Once the group has gotten accustomed to these basketballs moving around the circle, throw out the volleyball. Tell the group that this ball, being the rabbit, can jump across the circle as well as move around the circle. Now all three balls will be moving in the circle. The object of the game is to avoid having the coyotes catch the rabbit, which occurs when a group member is holding the rabbit and is also passed one or both coyotes. If one coyote catches the rabbit, the game stops momentarily and the group member who was holding the rabbit must tell something about himself. If both coyotes catch the rabbit, the game pauses and the rest of the group creates a question for the group member who was holding the rabbit to answer.

NOTES: ▶

If this game is played in the group room, put any breakables, like lamps or vases, away for safekeeping. Playing this game in a gymnasium or other recreation area is preferable because sometimes the playing can get a little wild. Another idea would be to use softer and lighter balls, such as beach balls or foam rubber balls.

MATERIALS: ▶

Two basketballs and one volleyball.

13
Guess Who I Am

GOALS: ▶

- Encourage honest communication
- Identify inaccuracies in self-perception
- Increase self-esteem

DESCRIPTION: ▶

Students write two brief personality sketches—the first concerning how they view themselves, and the second how they think the rest of the group views them. After guessing the correct identity of the first sketches, the group discusses the second sketches.

DIRECTIONS: ▶

Ask group members to write brief personality sketches about themselves. This short, one- or two-paragraph sketch should describe their mannerisms, how they interact with others, common moods, likes and dislikes, and so on. Once they've finished the first sketch, ask them to write another similar sketch on the bottom half of the paper, but this second sketch should focus on how they think the rest of the support group views them. In short, what do they think other students in the group think about them.

    Once everyone has finished writing, collect the sketches and mix them up in a stack. Read the first sketch in the pile out loud to the group and ask them to guess who they think is the author. After all has guessed, identify the person who wrote the sketch and then read the second part—how this person thinks the rest of the group sees her—to the group. As you read the second sketch, pause after each specific point and ask the group if they agree or disagree. For example, if this group member wrote "My support group thinks I am shy and quiet," ask the group if they agree: "Do all of you see Kathy as shy and quiet?"

    After reading the entire second sketch, ask the group to make additions to the sketch that the author didn't include—"Well, Kathy didn't say anything about how she always tries to help other people in the group when they are feeling down," for example. Follow this same routine for every group members' set of personality sketches.

MATERIALS:

Paper and pencils.

14
One Thing I Like About You

GOALS: ▶
- Encourage the giving and receiving of compliments
- Allow students to take risks in a safe environment
- Increase self-esteem

DESCRIPTION: ▶
Each group member gives a compliment to one group member who is chosen to be the focus of attention. Every student is given the opportunity to receive compliments from the rest of the group.

DIRECTIONS: ▶
Discuss the importance of self-esteem with the group, pointing out that though it's sometimes embarrassing to be given compliments, it sure makes us feel good. And it's important to feel good about ourselves, that we matter, that we have something to offer.

Choose someone to be the center of attention and then proceed around the circle, asking everybody to give a compliment to this particular student. When all have shared something, pick someone else (or ask for volunteers) to be the focus and repeat the sharing until everyone has had a chance to be the center of attention.

After everyone has received compliments, discuss the group members' reactions to being the focus of so many compliments. Encourage them to think about how they typically react to compliments they receive from family and friends.

QUESTIONS: ▶
- How did it feel to be given these compliments?
- Was it harder to give them or to receive them?
- Would it be okay to ask friends or family to give you some compliments when you are feeling down? Why or why not?
- Are you given compliments by family or friends?

NOTES: ▶
This isn't an activity for a group in its beginning stages. In fact, this activity won't even work in some groups that have been meeting for a long time because of the personal risk involved. When this activity does work, though, it's wonderfully effective at providing an avenue for group members to give each other sincere and powerful compliments.

MATERIALS: ▶
None required.

15
Eavesdropping

GOALS: ▶
- Discover new solutions to students' problems
- Encourage feedback from the group

DESCRIPTION: ▶ One group member sits outside the circle while the remainder of the group discusses his problems and possible solutions within his hearing distance.

DIRECTIONS: ▶ After explaining this activity to the group, ask for a volunteer. Inform the group that everyone will get a turn. Ask the volunteer to take her chair and sit some five feet outside the group circle with her back to the group. Tell her that she can listen to the conversation within the group, but that she can't respond until after they're finished and have invited her back to the circle.

Now, with her removed from the circle, ask the rest of the group to discuss this person: her family situation, the things about her that they appreciate, the things about her that concern them, what they think she should do to improve her situation.

When they are finished, ask her to rejoin the circle, allowing her to respond to the group's suggestions if she wishes. Discourage defensive justifications, however, reminding her that this is simply opinions of other group members and she is free to take what she likes and leave the rest (as they say in a number of twelve-step programs).

Use the rest of the session for other group members to be the focus of attention.

NOTES: ▶ You may wish to place the student being discussed behind a screen. This additional anonymity for the rest of the group encourages them to share their thoughts honestly. At times you may need to steer the conversation back towards a constructive focus if group members make inappropriate comments in an attempt to be humorous.

MATERIALS: ▶ None required.

16
My Secret Pal

GOALS: ▶

- Encourage group unity
- Build self-esteem
- Encourage students to be observant of others
- Provide evaluation of growth and learning

DESCRIPTION: ▶

Students are anonymously assigned to another member of the group. Everyone's task is to observe their secret pal discreetly, and then, after at least several sessions, give their pal his or her observations.

DIRECTIONS: ▶

Write each group member's name on a separate slip of paper and place them in a hat, or face down on a table. Ask group members to draw a slip, but not to share the name they draw with anyone else. After drawing names, tell the group that they are to observe their secret pal during future group sessions, looking for positive changes, such as risks taken or feelings being shared. They should do this discreetly, though, so that nobody knows who their secret pal is.

At some point during the last few sessions of the group experience, ask group members to reveal their partner's name and to share what they have observed. A student might have noticed that her partner was shy at first but eventually opened up and started sharing lots of feelings, or a secret pal might have observed that his partner always was helping others and putting everybody at ease.

QUESTIONS: ▶

- What did you notice about your secret pal?
- Did your secret pal suspect you were observing her?
- How has your secret pal changed during the course of this group?

You may wish to make the observation phase of this activity span the entire length of the group experience. The revelation of secret pal identities and the sharing of observations can be a great closing activity. Regardless of how many sessions you elect to span, it is best not to assign secret pals until the group is comfortable and familiar with each other, perhaps no earlier than the third or fourth session.

MATERIALS: ▶

Slips of paper.

17
Group Inventory Checklist

GOALS: ▶
- Confront problematic group dynamics
- Encourage self-inventory
- Promote positive group dynamics

DESCRIPTION: ▶
Students discuss questions on a checklist in order to assess the health of their support group as a whole.

DIRECTIONS: ▶
Explain to the group that just as we individually need to ask ourselves how we are doing from time to time, so does the group as a whole. Give the checklist (see following page) to a member of the group and ask her to choose a question for the group to discuss. If a group discussion doesn't naturally occur, you may ask each group member in turn to answer the specific question before proceeding with the next question. Let everyone have a chance to choose a question for the group to answer.

NOTES: ▶
As the group leader, it's appropriate for you also to answer questions put to the group. It's best to add your comments after everyone else has spoken except for those occasions when the group is hesitant to share their thoughts about a particular question, such as "Are there cliques in our group?"

MATERIALS: ▶
Group Inventory Checklist.

Group Inventory Checklist

1. Does our group help us?

2. Is our group enjoyable?

3. Do we encourage everyone to participate?

4. Does our group feel safe?

5. Does everyone participate in group, or do some members just take up space?

6. Do our group leaders do a good job at helping us?

7. Are there things we should be talking about but don't?

8. Do we spend too much time on some subjects?

9. Is anyone made fun of in group?

10. Are group rules being broken?

11. Are there cliques in our group?

12. Is there something that the group leader isn't doing that should be done?

13. Do people interrupt each other?

14. Do we volunteer information, or do we wait for the group leader to ask us?

15. What is great about our group?

16. How could we improve our group?

18
Worksheet Summary

GOALS: ▶

- Summarize the work completed by group members
- Provide written feedback regarding students' chemical use

DIRECTIONS: ▶

During the course of the group, collect all worksheets completed by group members. Reassure them you will be giving the worksheets back to them at the end of the group experience. Create a summary sheet that has room for your impressions for each activity that included a worksheet (see the following page for an example).

With the collected worksheets at hand, prepare a summary sheet for each group member. This is one more opportunity for you to share your thoughts and concerns about a student's chemical use, as well as other concerns. Staple the summary sheet on top of the student's worksheets.

Reserve one session of group to hand back the worksheet packets. Give the group time to read through their packets. Then with a particular student having the "hot seat", ask other group members to voice their impression of this group member's life-style and chemical use. "Tony, I think that you're really in trouble with your pot smoking and I wish you'd try to quit," for example. You may wish to proceed in a circular fashion so that everybody shares. After everyone else has voiced their opinions, then you share your concerns. Don't be afraid to speak your mind. This is the culmination of weeks of group and now is the time to lay it on the line. Before going on to the next group member, ask this group member to address the concerns raised by answering the following questions:

QUESTIONS: ▶

- What is your reaction to what the rest of the group is telling you?
- Do you think that you have a problem with chemicals? Explain.
- What are you willing to do about this?

NOTES: ▶

If the group member who's in the "hot seat" interrupts to defend himself, ask him to listen to what everyone has to say, and then he will be given ample time to speak.

MATERIALS: ▶

None required.

Worksheet Summary

This is a summary of many of the activities that you completed during this group. Beside each activity title is your group leaders' comments and impressions about your worksheet.

1   Interview Exercise

2   History of My Chemical Use

3   Chemicals and Feelings

4   Chemicals and Defenses

5   Consequences of Chemical Use

6   Is There Chemical Dependence in My Family?

Additional comments:

19
Group Evaluations

GOALS: ▶
- Solicit feedback from students about their group experiences
- Improve the effectiveness of support groups for future students
- Collect data regarding the impact of the group experience

DESCRIPTION: ▶ Group members complete written anonymous evaluations of their group experience.

DIRECTIONS: ▶ Hand out the evaluation worksheets (see following page), stressing to group members that they shouldn't write their names on the evaluations and that they should answer the questions honestly. Let them know that their feedback will be used to make the group experience better next time around for new students who join a support group.

NOTES: ▶ There are several different ways in which you can get these evaluations completed by group members, each having their own benefits and drawbacks. Perhaps the most popular and obvious way is to reserve the last ten minutes of the final group session to complete the worksheets. The drawback to this method is that this is a time when the group is feeling very emotional and intimate, and then you give them paperwork to complete (think about how much you detest writing evaluations after a long workshop). Instead, you could hand the worksheets out as they are leaving and ask them to return them when they are finished, but some students will forget or lose their worksheets. In this case, if there is academic credit being given for group attendance, you could reserve the final credit until the evaluations have been returned.

MATERIALS: ▶ **Group Evaluation** worksheets.

Group Evaluation

TO ALL GROUP MEMBERS:

Would you please take a minute to fill out this evaluation of group? Do not put your name on this. Thank you.

1. Was your group a valuable experience for you?

    No   Somewhat   Yes

    1   2   3   4   5   6   7   8   9   10

2. How would you rate your group leaders' ability to lead group?

    Poor   Excellent

    1   2   3   4   5   6   7   8   9   10

3. How helpful was your group leader for you?

    Of little help   Very helpful

    1   2   3   4   5   6   7   8   9   10

4. List three things that you learned in group.

    1)

    2)

    3)

5. How did this group help you?

6. How could this group be improved?

20
Support Group Party

GOALS:

- Celebrate the time spent together in group
- Validate personal work students have accomplished
- Bring about closure to the group

DESCRIPTION:

The group members plan and then have a party during one of the last sessions of group.

DIRECTIONS:

Ask group members to plan a party for the following week of group. This party should take place during one of the last sessions of group, although there might be other times when it also would be appropriate, such as the week before Christmas break. Place most of the responsibility for the party on the group's shoulders. They should decide who will be responsible for bringing music, refreshments, and what will happen during the party, such as playing games or listening to music.

NOTES: ▶

Some groups can't handle unstructured time well. If this is the case in your group, you might ask the group members to plan specific activities for the party.

MATERIALS: ▶

Refreshments, music, games.

Section B:
Feelings Awareness Activities

Basic communication skills, an understanding of our feelings, and recognition of who we are and what we want are fundamental to emotional health and a happy life. Since such self-awareness is difficult, most students in your group have discovered a seemingly easy way out, alcohol and other drugs. That's because chemicals are a salve for many hurts: low self-esteem, poor communication skills, loneliness, family dysfunction, physical or sexual abuse.

Most members of your group either lost their self-awareness through extensive chemical use, or they never knew themselves to begin with. Regardless, the activities in this section are designed to bring clarity and a realistic self-picture by focusing on feelings, attitudes, and past experiences. When they can see themselves more clearly, group members will understand what they need to change about themselves.

21
Ten Different Feelings

GOALS: ▶
- Identify personal defenses
- Encourage discussion of secret feelings

DESCRIPTION: ▶

Group members use a worksheet to categorize feelings as either simple or difficult to share.

DIRECTIONS: ▶

Ask group members to list some feelings that are easy to talk about; then ask them to list feelings that are really hard to talk about. Once they're familiar with this distinction, pass out the **Ten Different Feelings** worksheet (see following page). After they've had time to complete the worksheet, go around the circle and ask group members to share what they've written. Time permitting, ask them to relate an instance when they used a defense to cover up a feeling listed on their worksheet.

MATERIALS: ▶

Ten Different Feelings worksheet.

Ten Different Feelings

In the blanks provided, list ten different feelings you're familiar with. Then next to each feeling word you wrote, tell why the feeling is easy or difficult to reveal to other people.

■ Five feelings easy for me to reveal to others are:

1: _____

2: _____

3: _____

4: _____

5: _____

■ Five feelings difficult for me to reveal to others are:

1: _____

2: _____

3: _____

4: _____

5: _____

22
My Two Sides

Stage: 2-3
Challenge:
   MODERATE
Grades: ALL

GOALS: ▶
- Identify personal defenses
- Encourage discussion of secret feelings

DESCRIPTION: ▶

Group members explore the differences between their public and private feelings by labeling these feelings on an outline of their body.

DIRECTIONS: ▶

Ask group members to draw a large outline shape of themselves on newsprint. If the newsprint is large enough, they can lie down on the paper and have a friend trace their body on the paper. Inside the figure they should detail the feelings they keep to themselves and outside the figure, the feelings they reveal to the world around them. After everyone has done this, the disparity between the inside and outside should be discussed.

QUESTIONS: ▶
- What feelings do you have hidden inside?
- How do you present yourself to your family? to your friends?
- Why is there a difference between your inside feelings and your outside feelings?
- Why are some feelings harder to share than others?

NOTES: ▶

If you are instructing group members to draw their actual body outlines, be sensitive to possible uncomfortable feelings of a group member who is overweight.

MATERIALS: ▶

Large sheets of newsprint or bulletin board paper and markers.

23
Feelings Card Game

GOALS: ▶
- Increase awareness of feelings
- Develop communication skills

DESCRIPTION: ▶ Students select feelings cards representing their personality.

DIRECTIONS: ▶ This game uses the cards that come in the **Stamp Game** kit (see Resources section). Lay out the feelings cards in stacks in the center of the group circle. Call on group members to explain each of the eight feelings listed on the cards. Now ask students to take any number of cards from the piles to demonstrate the feelings they have inside. For example, a student might have a large pile of angry cards, a few guilt cards and one fear card. After everyone has had time to build their stack of cards, ask the group to discuss their stack of cards with the group by explaining why, for example, they have so many angry cards and what the fear cards are for. Additional game variations are provided in the **Stamp Game** kit.

NOTES: ▶ It is also possible to make your own set of feelings cards by cutting out cards from various colors of stiff paper and writing feelings words on them. You may wish to make this a group project.

MATERIALS: ▶ **Stamp Game** kit. (See Resources section).

24
Five Familiar Feelings

GOALS: ▶
- Identify the connection between feelings and behaviors
- Pinpoint troublesome feelings

DESCRIPTION: ▶ Group members describe specific situations that produce certain feelings and what they do with those feelings.

DIRECTIONS: ▶ Begin a discussion focusing on feelings by asking everyone in the group to each name a particular feeling that he or she has a difficult time handling. Point out to them that this is natural. Everyone handles some feelings better than others. Some can't deal with loneliness well; others get all bent out of shape when they are feeling angry.

Pass out the **Five Familiar Feelings** worksheet (see following page) for group members to complete. When they are finished, spend the remaining time discussing their answers. Be sure to ask for specific examples. Jeanette might have written that when she's feeling lonely she doesn't know what to do with herself, but through insisting that she identify specific examples she will begin to realize that it's when she's lonely that she ends up drunk. It is the specific, not the general, that will begin to make inroads into the confusion of group members.

MATERIALS: ▶ **Five Familiar Feelings** worksheet.

Five Familiar Feelings

For each of the five feelings below, first describe a typical situation that would lead to that feeling. Then give both a helpful as well as a harmful example of what you might do when you are feeling that way.

I feel happy when _____

When I'm feeling happy I . . .

Helpful: _____

Harmful: _____

I feel sad when _____

When I'm feeling sad I . . .

Helpful: _____

Harmful: _____

I feel angry when _____

When I'm feeling angry I . . .

Helpful: _____

Harmful: _____

I feel bored when _____

When I'm feeling bored I . . .

Helpful: _____

Harmful: _____

I feel lonely when _____

When I'm feeling lonely I . . .

Helpful: _____

Harmful: _____

25
What Should I Do with My Feelings?

GOALS: ▶
- Explore different ways to cope with feelings
- Increase awareness of the variety of feelings

DESCRIPTION: ▶
Group members identify feelings that they struggle with and the group discusses different strategies to manage these feelings.

DIRECTIONS: ▶
Ask each group member to think of a particular feeling that he or she finds difficult to handle. (See Appendix A for a list of feelings you may want to read aloud). Ask them to write this feeling, as well as a personal example, on a small piece of paper. Collect these papers, mix them up, draw a slip from the pile and read the feeling and the example out loud. Ask everyone in turn to explain how they deal with this particular feeling, giving examples from their personal lives. After all have shared, read the next slip of paper and continue the activity in likewise fashion.

NOTES: ▶
Don't be afraid to point out additional methods for coping with feelings if the group fails to mention strategies you think are important.

MATERIALS: ▶
Small pieces of paper, **Feelings List** (See Appendix A).

26
Personality Profile

GOALS: ▶
- Identify personality traits
- Help students understand their personality

DESCRIPTION: ▶
Students complete a worksheet that helps them understand the strengths and weaknesses of their personalities.

DIRECTIONS: ▶
Begin this session by challenging group members to describe their personalities. Most likely they will struggle with this, as it's a difficult task for all of us.

Explain to the group that despite its difficulty, this is an important question to wrestle with. We all need to know about ourselves. Are we outgoing or reserved, happy or sad, lonely or the life of the party, quick to anger or easygoing? Give everyone a copy of the **Personality Profile** worksheet (see following page) to complete. Once they have finished, spend the remaining time discussing their answers.

QUESTIONS: ▶
- Has your personality always been like it is now?
- If it has changed, when did it and why?
- Are you happy with your personality now?
- What would you change?
- How could you go about changing your personality?

MATERIALS: ▶
Personality Profile worksheet.

Personality Profile

Consider each set of opposite traits below and circle the number that best describes you. Once you have scored the fifteen traits, connect your circles with a line from top to bottom.

calm	1	2	3	4	5	6	nervous
popular	1	2	3	4	5	6	loner
expressive	1	2	3	4	5	6	inhibited
caring	1	2	3	4	5	6	indifferent
aggressive	1	2	3	4	5	6	compliant
patient	1	2	3	4	5	6	impatient
self-disciplined	1	2	3	4	5	6	impulsive
trustworthy	1	2	3	4	5	6	untrustworthy
happy	1	2	3	4	5	6	sad
honest	1	2	3	4	5	6	dishonest
confident	1	2	3	4	5	6	insecure
mellow	1	2	3	4	5	6	angry
abstinent	1	2	3	4	5	6	heavy user
self-aware	1	2	3	4	5	6	unaware
motivated	1	2	3	4	5	6	procrastinator

27
Life Maps

GOALS: ▶
- Validate personal experiences
- Establish group unity
- Familiarize leaders with students' family histories

DESCRIPTION: ▶ Students draw a timeline of their lives that illustrates their past experiences.

DIRECTIONS: ▶ Pass out blank sheets of newsprint and markers and give the students an entire group session to draw the chronological history of their lives—from when they were born to the present. They should include anything that's significant to them: moving, parent's divorce, Dad coming home drunk and yelling at everyone, first kiss, first time they smoked marijuana, changing schools, and so on. Undoubtedly, they will want to know how to record this information so discuss a few examples: linear *progression*—construct a timeline, placing significant events in chronological order; *boxed captions*—draw squares and sketch different scenes in each; *journal entries*—some students won't want to draw, so let them write out the events and their feelings (see following page for a sample Life Map). Encourage everyone to be creative and make sure they understand the importance of including their own feelings associated with the past events.

Several sessions of group following should be used to share these life maps. Ask two other members of the group to hold the student's life map for the rest of the group to see while he explains the contents. Give each member a reasonable amount of time to discuss their life map with the group. If students are hesitant to share, or if they skip over things, slow them down by asking questions. Typically, group members will want to give only superficial information: "This happened, and then that happened, and then my brother. . . ." This isn't what you want. Instead, ask questions which encourage the identification and expression of feelings: "How did you feel inside when you got kicked out of school?" "What was the feeling when your Mom left your Dad?" Encourage other group members to ask questions too; this will set the stage for the group to function as a group rather than the leader always asking the questions.

NOTES: ▶ You should cover between two and three life maps each session of group. More than three life maps in one session means you are moving too quickly; instead, ask additional questions and encourage the students to talk in more depth. Less than two means the students are sharing quite a bit, but it also means that you will be dealing with life maps for many weeks to come.

MATERIALS: ▶ Large sheets of newsprint, markers, or crayons.

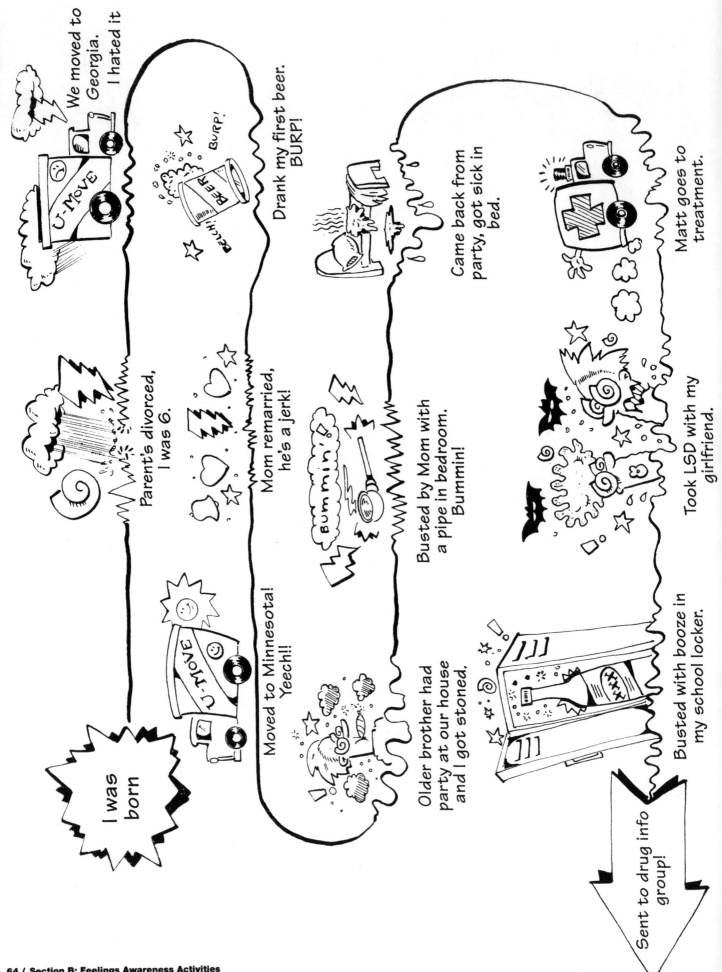

28
Journaling

GOALS: ▶
- Encourage students to reflect on their thoughts and feelings
- Increase self-awareness
- Strengthen writing skills

DESCRIPTION: ▶

Group members are taught how to record their thoughts and feelings in a journal.

DIRECTIONS: ▶

Introduce the concept of journaling to the group by explaining the positive aspects of keeping a journal:
- 1 - It helps you understand your own thoughts and feelings.
- 2 - It provides an avenue for expressing thoughts and feelings that you wouldn't ever share with others.
- 3 - You can read back through previous entries and see how your feelings and problems have changed over time.

Tell the group that each week, the first five minutes of group will be set aside for writing in journals. Make sure the group members understand that they can write whatever they wish, and that nobody will read their journals. They are private. They can keep their journals in the group room or, if they want to write more during the week, they can take the journals with them and bring them back each week.

NOTES: ▶

You may wish to expand on this activity. Here are several different options to consider:
- 1 - After the group has finished writing each week, ask if anybody would like to share what he or she has written.
- 2 - Near the last session of the support group, set aside one session for students to read through their journals and then discuss what has changed during the course of the group sessions as evidenced by their journal entries.

Regardless of how this activity is handled, make sure you show group members that you take their privacy seriously by carefully collecting and putting their journals away in a safe place each week.

MATERIALS: ▶

Spiral notebooks or sheets of lined paper stapled together (one sheet for each session of group).

29
Whole Person Wheel

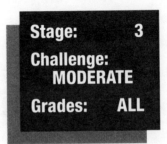

GOALS: ▶
- Create awareness of personal needs
- Help students understand their personalities

DESCRIPTION: ▶ Students respond to a number of sentence stems challenging them to think about who they are and what they need.

DIRECTIONS: ▶ Pass out sheets of newsprint and ask group members to write the word "I" in the center and draw a small circle around it. Then they should draw eight equally-spaced lines outward to the edge of the paper from the center, like the spokes of a wheel. Towards the middle, they should write the following words, one in each section: want, am, have, love, hate, fear, wish, need. Once done, ask group members to spend some time thinking about and then filling in the triangle sections with appropriate endings to the sentence stems. I need . . . people who care about me, love from my family; I wish . . . I could graduate this year, Liz would go out with me. Encourage them to fill in as many examples as they can for each section. Reserve some time at the end of the session to share answers within the group.

MATERIALS: ▶ Sheets of newsprint, markers and pencils.

30
Fantasy Islands

GOALS: ▶
- Clarify personal values
- Identify personally important people and places
- Encourage discussion of present circumstances

DESCRIPTION: ▶
Group members draw their own island country, deciding who and what to include. The islands are discussed when everyone has finished drawing.

DIRECTIONS: ▶
After handing out large sheets of newsprint, tell group members to draw the outline of a large island that will be their own. After they have drawn the island's shape, let them know that, since this is their island, they are in charge of who and what is on the island. And since this is a fantasy island, anything goes: Candy trees, rivers of warm water, a house built out of gold, a remote section of the island for their parents to live, no rules, lots of rules. Encourage them to be creative (see following page for an example).
Save some time at the end of the session for group members to discuss their islands.

QUESTIONS: ▶
- Who is welcome on your island?
- What is especially important about your island?
- What aspects of your island are similar to your life now?
- What aspects of your island are different from your life now?
- What does Julie's island tell us about her? (Ask the rest of the group.)

NOTES: ▶
If the group seems hesitant or unsure of this task, it's best for you, as the group leader, to just start drawing your own island—soon the others will follow suit.

MATERIALS: ▶
Large sheets of newsprint, markers and crayons.

FANTASY ISLAND

(where me and all
my friends hang out)

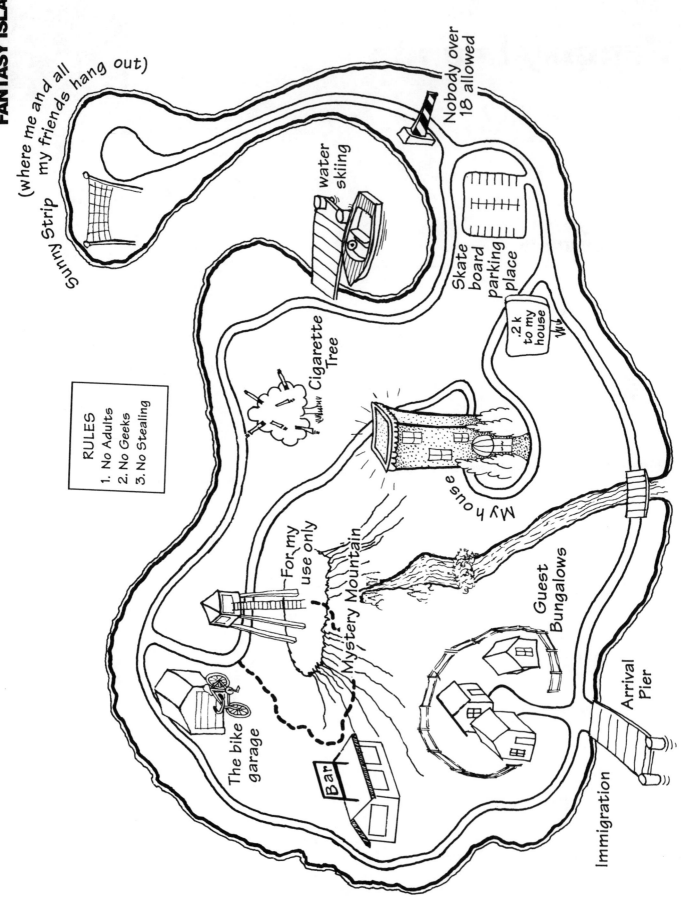

Sunny Strip

Nobody over
18 allowed

water
skiing

Skate
board
parking
place

.2 k
to my
house

Cigarette
Tree

RULES
1. No Adults
2. No Geeks
3. No Stealing

My house

For my
use only

Mystery Mountain

The bike garage

Bar

Guest
Bungalows

Immigration

Arrival
Pier

31
Draw Your School

GOALS: ▶
- Communicate feelings and attitudes about school
- Explore relationship between school and personal issues

DESCRIPTION: ▶

Group members draw personal impressions of their school, including their classrooms, teachers, and other students.

DIRECTIONS: ▶

Ask group members to close their eyes and imagine their school, classrooms, and the teachers they interact with throughout the day. Ask them to concentrate on their emotional responses to their school day such as how it feels when they are waiting for the bus in the morning, at a pep-fest, in a boring class, spending a few minutes talking with the teacher after class, or standing in the halls while everyone is rushing past.

After they have an emotional picture of their school experience in mind, hand out large sheets of newsprint and ask them to draw their school and the significant people that they interact with there. Point out that their drawings should focus on this emotional picture—they shouldn't try to make their drawings a true physical representation of the school (see following page for an example).

Once everyone has finished, spend the remaining time discussing these drawings.

QUESTIONS: ▶
- What feeling words would you use to describe your school?
- What aspects of school do you like the most? the least?
- Are there adults in the school whom you could talk to if you had a problem? Who are they?
- Has your impression of school changed over the years? Why or why not?
- What can you change to make school a more positive experience for yourself?

MATERIALS: ▶

Newsprint and markers.

32
My Song

GOALS: ▶
- Clarify personal values
- Identify personally important people and places
- Encourage discussion of current issues

DESCRIPTION: ▶

Group members bring lyrics of a favorite song to group and, after reading them out loud, discuss why the lyrics are important to them.

DIRECTIONS: ▶

The week previous to this session, ask group members to choose a favorite song and bring the lyrics to group. Tell them they'll be asked to explain the song's personal significance.

    The following week ask group members to read the lyrics to their songs out loud and then explain to the group why the song is important to them.

QUESTIONS: ▶
- Why did you choose this song?
- What do you think this song's message is?
- How does this song make you feel?
- Why is this song important to you?

NOTES: ▶

Be aware of the fact that some students might bring lyrics that contain profane language or lyrics promoting sexism, racism, or other offensive actions. If you feel uncomfortable including these topics in group discussion, you may not want to use this activity. Another option would be to say something like "Choose a favorite song that doesn't contain any objectionable language or content."

MATERIALS: ▶

None required.

33
Johari Window

GOALS: ▶

- Increase awareness of communication patterns
- Reinforce appropriate levels of communication

DESCRIPTION: ▶

After hearing a brief presentation about the different levels of communication, students identify which levels of communication they use with various people in their lives.

DIRECTIONS: ▶

Using a blackboard, draw and explain a Johari window to the group (see following page for information). Ask group members to give examples of communication for each of the four windows to make sure they understand. Then pass out sheets of paper and ask them to draw a large Johari window, writing several personal communication examples in squares 1 and 2. Point out to them, if necessary, why they can't complete squares 3 and 4. When everyone is finished, ask them to share their windows. After a student has shared what she wrote in squares 1 and 2, ask the rest of the group to offer information for this student to record in square 3.

NOTES: ▶

When group members are offering information to put in the third window for a student, make sure that the group is being gentle. Sometimes group members, though not intending harm, can offer hurtful information about another group member's "blind" window.

MATERIALS: ▶

Paper.

For Your Information...

Johari Window

I know

1. OPEN	2. PRIVATE
3. BLIND	4. UNKNOWN

You know

Johari window is a convenient model for both understanding and explaining communication dynamics between human beings. And this communication refers to much more than language. Body language, clothing styles, sounds, and degree of eye contact also convey much of the information that is exchanged during the communication process.

The first window is open. It includes information that both you and I know, such as hair color, gender, and the like. Depending on the relationship you have with the person you're communicating with, the open window will include other information: your name, what you like to do in your free time, where you live.

The second window contains our secrets, the things that we know about ourselves that other people don't. Things we've done that we're ashamed of, some of our fears and dreams, and some of the feelings we have about our parent's drinking problem all fit in our private window.

The third window contains all the information other people know about us, but that we ourselves don't know, like what we look like when we walk, little gestures we often use when we're speaking, or that we are very quiet. The only way we can learn about our third window is for others to share this information with us. Sometimes this information is difficult to share or hear.

The fourth window contains the information about us that neither we nor anybody else knows about us. Unconscious thoughts and our night dreams are examples of information that belong in our unknown window.

34
The Grieving Process

GOALS: ▶
- Teach the stages of grieving
- Prepare students for possible grief reactions when they quit abusing chemicals

DESCRIPTION: ▶
Students learn about the stages of grieving and discuss their possible grief reactions to abstaining from mind altering chemicals.

DIRECTIONS: ▶
Begin this session by making a presentation that conveys the five stages of the grieving process (see following page for more information). Make certain they all understand this process by asking the group to describe possible grief reactions for a hypothetical loss that the group invents such as a family member dying.

When this concept and its stages are well understood by the group, ask them to imagine themselves quitting their use of all mind altering chemicals and their personal grief reactions. For example: Ken might see himself becoming very angry (anger stage) that he can't use any longer, especially when he sees his friends going off to a party; Nancy thinks she would fight the fact that she even needs to quit, instead wanting to cut down on how often she drinks (bargaining stage).

Once you have given them a few minutes to contemplate this, use the remaining time to share these grief reactions.

MATERIALS: ▶
None required.

For Your Information...

Grief is a reaction to any heartfelt loss. Probably the first example that comes to mind is the death of a loved one, but there are many other examples, such as moving away, leaving adolescence, ending a relationship.

Young people who abuse alcohol and other drugs do so for myriad reasons, but it's safe to say that the mind-altering chemicals do something for them, be it making them feel popular, attractive, happy. Because alcohol and other drugs do this, chemically dependent people develop a love affair with alcohol and other drugs. When they quit this love affair, they will grieve the loss of identity, a group of friends, rituals, excitement, pleasure. Of course, they don't really lose these things—it just feels like it. Just as someone grieving over a divorce often feels there will never be anyone else in his life. It's important for young people struggling to quit using alcohol and other drugs to understand that it's normal for them to grieve the loss of this drug-centered life-style.

Grieving has stages, first identified by Elizabeth Kübler-Ross in her work with dying patients. Listed below are these five stages and the thoughts typical of someone who has been diagnosed terminally ill with cancer:

Denial - "No, it can't be true. I've just got the flu."
Anger -"These quack doctors don't know anything."
Bargaining -"I'll take my pills, but I'm never going to go through chemotherapy."
Depression -"What's the use in trying."
Acceptance -"I've got cancer but I'm going to enjoy every day I've got left."

A teenager who quits smoking pot might have this to say:

Denial - "I don't have a problem."
Anger -"Hey, get off my back—you're my problem!"
Bargaining -"I'll quit hanging around with Bill, but I'm still going to go to parties."
Depression -"I'm going to be the only straight kid in the entire school."
Acceptance -"As long as I stay clean and sober, I'm going to graduate from high school!"

These stages are experienced in sequence and it's common to return to a stage previously experienced. A young person might vacillate between denial, anger, and bargaining for a long time before moving into the last two stages. She might even jump back up into the first three briefly again. Grieving students will work through these stages differently and at their own pace.

Section C: Family Relations

Even though teenagers are very quick to point out the fact that they are not a child any longer, group members' families have much impact on their attitudes, feelings, and behaviors. Many young people in trouble with chemicals come from homes where a parent is chemically dependent. Chemical dependence is often called the family disease because it affects everyone in the family. Honest communication is blocked, emotional and sometimes even physical needs aren't met consistently, while the dynamics of denial force everyone to play the "there's nothing wrong here" game. Statistics clearly show that children of these chemically dependent parents are at a higher risk for developing the same disease.

Many other young people come from divorced and single-parent homes. Lack of same-sex role models and a single parent who's always at work make it easy for a young person to stray. Many children from divorced homes tearfully state they would much rather their parents stayed together rather than to "lose" Mom or Dad.

This isn't to say that it's always the parents' fault. Indeed, some chemically dependent young people are like tornadoes in an otherwise-healthy family. Regardless, it's important for the group leaders and group members to gain an understanding of what's going on at home. The activities in this section will help group members understand their own family dynamics better, and help them decide whether there is a problem with chemical dependence in their family.

35
Family Faces

GOALS: ▶
- Increase awareness of family dynamics
- Assess specific relationships within students' families

DESCRIPTION: ▶
Students complete a worksheet by drawing expressive faces for, and describing the relationship with, each member of their families.

DIRECTIONS: ▶
Hand out the **Family Faces** worksheet (see following page) and ask them to draw expressive features for each blank face. When they are finished with the faces, they should follow the instructions for the blank lines next to each face. After everyone has finished the worksheet, ask them to share their answers with the group.

QUESTIONS: ▶
- Do the moods of your family members change often? Why is this?
- Can you read the differing moods of your family?
- Which family members do you feel close to? Which ones are difficult for you to spend time with?

NOTES: ▶
When students are living with a stepparent, they might ask, for example, if they should designate their biological father or their stepfather (or Mom's live-in boyfriend) as "Dad." Instruct them to make their own choices, but to place the person they didn't select as "Dad" in the "other family" section of the worksheet.

MATERIALS: ▶
Family Faces worksheet.

Family Faces

FAMILY FACES

	words that describe this person	words that describe your feelings about this person
MOM		
DAD		
BROTHERS & SISTERS		
OTHER FAMILY		

36
Family Collage

GOALS: ▶

- Describe students' families
- Explore feelings related to family issues

DESCRIPTION: ▶

Students make a collage depicting their families and family issues using pictures cut from magazines.

DIRECTIONS: ▶

Place a large stack of magazines in the center of the group circle. After giving everyone scissors, glue, and a sheet of construction paper, ask group members to page through the magazines and cut out pictures or words that describe their families, the problems their families experience, and the students' reaction to their families. They can either paste on pictures and words as they find them, or first cut out all of the pictures they will use and then begin to assemble the collage. Once the collages are finished, the remaining time can be spent discussing them.

QUESTIONS: ▶

- What kind of feelings are represented in your collage?
- What are the problems in your family?
- What would you change in your family?
- Where are you in your collage?

NOTES: ▶

You may wish to make this activity span two sessions—the first for making the collage and the second for group discussion.

MATERIALS: ▶

Wide variety of magazines representing cultural diversity, sheets of construction paper, scissors, and bottles of white glue.

37
Divorce Discussion

GOALS: ▶
- Encourage honest discussion about divorce
- Identify problems and solutions related to divorce

DESCRIPTION: ▶
The group room is split into two halves representing yes and no. The leader asks discussion questions and group members indicate their response by standing in either half of the room.

DIRECTIONS: ▶
Use masking tape to make a line on the group room floor. Tell students that one side is the "yes zone" and the other is the "no zone." Furthermore, the farther from the line they stand, the more strongly they are responding to the question. Begin the activity by reading one of the questions from the divorce discussion question list (see following page) and then asking group members to position themselves in the room according to their responses. After everyone is still, ask group members to explain their answer to the question. Encourage group discussion rather than short responses to the question.

MATERIALS: ▶
Discussion Questions.

Divorce Discussion Questions

- Is it hard on children when their parents get divorced?

- Should parents stay together for the sake of the children?

- Should parents decide whom the children must live with?

- Is a drinking or drug problem a good reason to get divorced?

- Does a divorce solve the problems the parents were having?

- Should parents have to see a marriage counselor before they get divorced?

- Should a parent be denied the chance to see his or her children?

- Should custody rights usually be in favor of the mother?

- If your parents are divorced, was the divorce difficult for you? If your parents aren't divorced, would a divorce be difficult for you?

- If your parents are divorced, are you glad they are? If your parents aren't divorced, do you wish they were?

Is There Chemical Dependence in My Family?

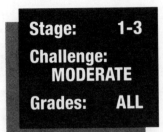

Stage: 1-3
Challenge: MODERATE
Grades: ALL

GOALS:

- Identify group members with chemically dependent families
- Encourage honest appraisal of the problem
- Increase understanding of students' degree of risk

DESCRIPTION: ▶

Group members complete a short questionnaire that focuses on how children are affected by a parent's chemical dependence. The remainder of the session is spent discussing the group members' answers.

DIRECTIONS: ▶

Pass out the questionnaires (see following page) and ask students to answer each question honestly. After everyone has finished, ask students to share their answers with the rest of the group.

NOTES: ▶

Being mindful of the time remaining, ask group members for examples rather than simply "yes" or "no" answers. For example, with question #1 you could ask, "Why are you concerned?" or "What bothers you about this person's drinking?"

In an average Drug Information Group, it's common for 50 percent of the group members to be experiencing chemical dependence in their families. This session is an excellent opportunity to reinforce the high-risk nature of group members who both abuse chemicals and are children of chemically dependent parents.

MATERIALS:

Questionnaire.

Questionnaire

CHECK YES OR NO TO THE FOLLOWING QUESTIONS

	YES	NO
1. Are you concerned about a parent's, relative's, or close friend's chemical use?	☐	☐
2. Do you spend a lot of time thinking about this person's chemical use?	☐	☐
3. Have you ever thought that this person has a problem with his or her chemical use?	☐	☐
4. Do you stay out of the house as much as possible because of this person's chemical use?	☐	☐
5. Are you afraid to upset this person because it may cause him or her to use more chemicals?	☐	☐
6. Do you feel that no one at home really loves you or cares what happens to you?	☐	☐
7. Are you afraid or embarrassed to bring your friends home because of a family member's chemical use?	☐	☐
8. Do you tell lies to cover up for this person's chemical use?	☐	☐
9. Have you ever wanted to talk to somebody about this person's chemical use?	☐	☐
10. Is your schoolwork suffering because of this person's chemical use?	☐	☐

39
The Inheritance

Stage: 3
Challenge: MODERATE
Grades: ALL

GOALS: ▶
- Increase awareness of genetic predisposition to chemical dependence
- Encourage students to abstain from alcohol and other drugs

DESCRIPTION: ▶
Group members are presented information concerning their genetic and environmental predisposition to chemical dependence. This information is presented through a combination of video, lecture, and discussion. Alternative activities to a video are also discussed.

DIRECTIONS: ▶
Use the information on the next page to make a short presentation about the nature of genetic predisposition. Encourage an interactive approach by asking their opinions (for example, what percent of children with chemically dependent parents become chemically dependent themselves?) before you outline the facts. Discussion can stem from a variety of questions: Is chemical dependence passed on genetically, is it learned through modeling parents' drinking behaviors, or does it stem from the fact that these kids often have traumatic childhoods? Can the students identify a history of chemical dependence in their extended families? Do the group members think they're at risk? Why or why not? Do they use mind-altering chemicals now?

You may also want to begin this activity by showing the video *My Father's Son* (see Resources section). After the video, ask group members what they think will happen to the teenager in the video. Does the son have a problem with chemicals? What are the chances he will in the future?

Next, outline some basic facts about genetic predisposition (see information on following page) and begin a discussion in which group members connect this information with their own families. Are there histories of chemical dependence in their families? Do they think that they are at risk for becoming chemically dependent? Why or why not?

NOTES: ▶

The video, while not crucial to this activity, is an excellent vehicle for presenting the concept of genetic predisposition.

MATERIALS: ▶

For Your Information, *My Father's Son* video (optional).

For Your Information . . .

Chemical Dependence — Learned or Inherited?

Much has been written concerning the relationship between parents' chemical dependence and their sons or daughters' chemical use. Everyone agrees that the children of parents who are chemically dependent are at high risk for becoming chemically dependent themselves. What isn't clear is exactly how this relationship is passed on from parent to child.

Genetic Predisposition: This position supports the idea that simply by having a biological parent who is chemically dependent, you are at risk for becoming chemically dependent. There is research demonstrating that children of alcoholics who are adopted into healthy families as infants still show high rates of alcoholism when they have grown up.

Common sense would also support the idea that, since children's primary role models are their parents, these children also become high risk simply by modeling what they see their parents doing—which is, in this case, a lot of drinking or using other drugs. The fact that every time their parent is troubled he or she drinks becomes a powerful, though harmful, lesson.

Environmental: Then there are those who point to the fact that these children grow up in turbulent, painful, and dysfunctional home environments. Simply put, these children have a painful childhood and carry these problems around with them, eventually turning to mind-altering chemicals for escape and relief.

All of this boils down to the classic nature vs. nurture controversy for which there are few simple answers. Currently, the majority believe that the answer is a combination of all three factors, each contributing to the amount of risk. Here are some current statistics:

- More than half of all alcoholics have an alcoholic parent.[1]
- Children of alcoholics are four times more likely than others to become alcoholics in the future.[2]
- Thirty percent of children with an alcoholic parent will marry an alcoholic.[3]

---

[1]Linda Christensen, *Facts, Feelings, Family and Friends* (Minneapolis: Johnson Institute, 1990).
[2]Woodside, M. "Children of Alcoholic Parents: Inherited and Psychosocial Influences." *Journal of Psychiatric Treatment and Evaluation* 5 (1983): 531-537.
[3]Claudia Black, "Innocent Bystanders at Risk: The Children of Alcoholics," *Alcoholism,* (January/February 1981): 22-26.

Section D: Chemical Dependence Information

There is perhaps no other disease that includes as much confusion, denial, and misinformation as does chemical dependence. After all, if a teenager can mistakenly believe she can't get pregnant the first time she has sex, imagine the potential for misinformation where chemical dependence is concerned. "This drug won't hurt you," "that drug is okay because my sister does it," "You can't get addicted to this stuff." Young people using alcohol and other drugs need correct relevant information about the effects of chemicals on their bodies, brains, and an understanding of the dynamics of both psychological as well as physical dependence.

But it must be relevant. We must tell them why we don't want them to drink or use other drugs. We must show them what can happen when someone gets caught up in the disease of chemical dependence. And all of this information must be presented on their level, in a way that is personalized to their situation.

The activities in this section present the information these young people need to know. Through these activities, they will begin to understand what the disease of chemical dependence is about, including the different stages one goes through. They will be challenged to explore the real reasons why people use chemicals, and what the chemicals do for them. The final activity in this section focuses on the relationship between drinking, blood-alcohol content, and drinking and driving, an important topic because alcohol-related car crashes are the leading cause of death for this age group.

40
Why Do People Use Chemicals?

GOALS:

- Explore reasons for using chemicals
- Help students identify why they use chemicals

DESCRIPTION:

Students identify different reasons why people use chemicals and discuss their reasons for abusing chemicals.

DIRECTIONS: ▶

Using the blackboard, ask group members to brainstorm all the different reasons that people use chemicals, such as to sleep better, to win friends, to forget, to reduce stress. When a student offers an example, ask her to describe a specific situation to both dramatize as well as clarify the example.

Once the list is complete (they should list at least twenty reasons), ask the group to look over the list carefully and decide which of these are also reasons for their using chemicals. Ask them to share their own reasons for using chemicals, again giving personal examples.

MATERIALS: ▶

None required.

41 Messages about Chemical Use

GOALS: ▶
- Increase awareness of manipulation by media
- Identify societal messages concerning chemical use

DESCRIPTION: ▶ Students make collages of ads that influence their attitudes about using chemicals.

DIRECTIONS: ▶ Place a large pile of general-interest magazines in the center of the group circle along with enough scissors and bottles of glue for everyone. Give everyone a sheet of newsprint and ask them to page through the magazines, cutting out advertisements and other messages that address chemical use. These messages may be either positive or negative. They should use these cut-outs to make a collage that reflects their impressions of societal messages about chemical use. Save some time at the end of the session to discuss the collages, asking students to explain their collages to the rest of the group.

QUESTIONS: ▶
- What messages are we given about chemical use?
- Do the messages differ according to the chemical?
- Which of these messages are true? Which are false?
- Do these messages affect your attitudes or behaviors?

NOTES: ▶ Talking about these collages is the important part of this activity. It's common for students to want to work on their collages right up to the end of the session, but you must save some time for discussion—even if they haven't finished. It's a good idea to sound a ten- and five-minute warning as they approach the end of the time available for working on the collages.

MATERIALS: ▶ Magazines, scissors, glue.

42
Physical and Psychological Addictions

GOALS: ▶
- Teach the difference between the two types of addiction
- Increase the understanding of the dynamics of addiction

DESCRIPTION: ▶
After you define the difference between the two types of addiction, students categorize a variety of mind-altering chemicals into either classification.

DIRECTIONS: ▶
Begin this session by making a brief presentation explaining the difference between physical and psychological addiction (see **For Your Information** on the following pages). Once this is well understood, ask a group member to name a mind-altering chemical, such as marijuana. Ask the group to decide whether or not marijuana is physical or psychologically addictive by discussion or voting. You may wish to designate one side of the room as physical and the other as psychological and instruct students to go to one side of the room or the other. Regardless of how this is done, be sure to encourage group members to explain their opinion. The discussion of the various effects that differing chemicals produce in the human body is what is most important here, not the correctness of their answers.

After the group has reached a consensus, give them the correct answer for the chemical in question. Ask for a different student to name a new chemical and again put the addiction question to the group. Repeat this for every chemical that the students can identify. If they miss any important ones on your list, help them out.

NOTES: ▶
Make sure you stress that the biggest problem associated with having an alcohol or other drug problem is psychological addiction.

MATERIALS: ▶
None required.

For Your Information . . .

Physical and Psychological Addictions

Any chemical that changes how we feel can be addicting. This includes anything from nicotine to alcohol, from sniffing glue to heroin. But, beyond the fact that you want to use the chemical more and more, what exactly does addiction mean? Is being a junkie the same as being a heavy cigarette smoker?

While the world of addiction research is truly complex, it's helpful to think of addictions as falling into one of two categories: physical addictions and psychological addictions. If a person regularly uses a substance that is physically addictive, that person's body will react negatively when he or she quits using this chemical. Depending on the particular drug, the size of the dose, the frequency of use, and the history of use, these withdrawal reactions can range from minor irritability to violent seizures.

If a substance is psychologically addictive, the need for the chemical is in the user's mind rather than the body. Here, withdrawal is in the form of anxiety, depression, and an expressed desperate need for the chemical. *Bear in mind that all drugs can be psychologically addictive and some are physically addictive as well.* For example, someone physically addicted to barbiturates is most likely psychologically addicted as well because he was using the chemical to change his feelings and became "hooked" on the drug's ability to do this. Along the way, after using the barbiturates regularly, his body also became physically addicted.

Despite what the television might portray, it's psychological addiction—the need to change one's thoughts and feelings— that's the most serious problem. If someone enters a residential treatment center physically addicted to alcohol—yes, alcohol is physically addictive—the first order of the day is to withdraw them safely from this physical addiction. The real heart of the treatment program, though, will be to deal with the psychological dependence. After all, it's the psychological need that is responsible for creating the physical addiction. This needs to be strongly stressed to group members, who will often remark, "Well, getting high is safe because you can't get hooked on it." The majority of teenagers who suffer from chemical dependence are not physically addicted to any chemical. They suffer from psychological addiction.

continued on next page

For Your Information...

continued

Here's a list of common mind-altering chemicals and their addiction classification:

	Psychologically addictive	Physically addictive
Alcohol	Yes (beer, wine, hard liquor)	Yes (possible serious withdrawal side effects)
Marijuana (pot, hashish, thai sticks)	Yes	No
Cocaine	Yes	Yes (high risk)
Hallucinogens (LSD, mushrooms, peyote, MDA, angel dust)	Yes	No
Amphetamines (speed, crystal, meth)	Yes	Yes
Tranquilizers (Valium, Librium)	Yes	Yes
Sedatives (Nembutal, Seconal)	Yes	Yes
Narcotics (codeine, morphine, heroin, Demerol, Percodan)	Yes	Yes (high potential)
Inhalants (glue, gasoline, White-out, solvents, rush, amyl nitrate)	Yes	No
Nicotine (cigarettes, chew, snuff)	Yes	Yes
Caffeine (coffee, No-Doz, diet pills, most soft drinks, chocolate)	Yes	No

43
The Chemical Quiz

GOALS: ▶
- Increase knowledge of chemicals
- Dispel myths about chemicals

DESCRIPTION: ▶
Group members break into teams and play a true or false game concerning chemical facts.

DIRECTIONS: ▶
Break the group into two teams and select a team captain. Read questions from the list provided on the following page to each group in turn. Encourage the group to discuss their answer before their team captain speaks. Correct answers are worth one point. If a team is incorrect, give the opposing team a chance to explain the correct answer. If their explanation is satisfactory, give them one point. When it is clear to you that none of the students can correctly answer the question, briefly explain the correct answer to the group before moving on.

NOTES: ▶
You may wish to make a stack of cards, with a question on one side and the answer on the back, so that group members can select their own questions.

MATERIALS: ▶
Questions List.

Questions List

1 Alcohol is a stimulant.   (False)
   (Alcohol is a depressant.)

2. Withdrawal from cocaine often creates deep depression   (True)

3. Inhalants can cause kidney damage.   (True)

4. Withdrawal from heroin is more severe than from alcohol.   (False)
   (Withdrawal from physical addiction to alcohol can produce dangerous
   side effects known as delirium tremens characterized by sweats, trembling,
   and frightening hallucinations.)

5. Regular users of stimulants often become paranoid.   (True)

6. Overdoses occur most frequently with narcotics.   (False)
   (Tranquilizers are the most common drug involved in overdoses.)

7. Nembutal and seconal are narcotics.   (False)
   (They are both sedatives.)

8. Nicotine reduces your heart rate and calms you down.   (False)
   (Nicotine accelerates your heart rate.)

9. You cannot overdose on alcohol.   (False)
   (As a depressant, it is possible to ingest enough alcohol to stop the
   nervous system's basic functions.)

10. Codeine is a physically addictive drug.   (True)

11. Alcohol use by pregnant mothers can cause mental retardation in
    their babies.   (True)

12. Heroin is the leading cause of drug-related deaths.   (False)
    (Alcohol causes the highest number of deaths because of related
    traffic fatalities.)

44
The Disease of Chemical Dependence

GOALS: ▶
- Help students understand chemical dependence is a disease
- Encourage students to find examples of chemical dependence in their personal lives

DESCRIPTION: ▶
After a brief presentation explaining the disease concept, group members break up into teams and discuss examples of chemical dependence they have witnessed.

DIRECTIONS: ▶
Begin this session by asking the group why it is that we refer to chemical dependence as a disease. After discussing this for a minute make a short presentation that covers the major points of the disease concept (see page 96 for more information).

After the group has a grasp of the major points of this disease, break the large group up into diads and give each team a copy of the worksheet on the following page to complete as a group. Both students should volunteer information when possible. When they are finished, bring the students back together and use the remaining time to discuss their answers.

MATERIALS: ▶
The Disease of Chemical Dependence worksheet.

The Disease of Chemical Dependence

Like other diseases such as cancer or diabetes, chemical dependence has recognizable and predictable characteristics. Using examples from your personal life, someone in your family, somebody you know, or even someone famous you've heard about, describe an example for each of the common characteristics listed below.

1. Chemical dependence is a primary disease.

2. Chemical dependence is a compulsive and obsessive disease.

3. Chemical dependence is a progressive disease.

4. Chemical dependence is a chronic disease.

5. Chemical dependence is a fatal disease.

6. Chemical dependence is a treatable disease.

For Your Information. . .

The Disease of Chemical Dependence

It used to be believed that chemical dependence was a sign of low self-control, lax morals, irresponsibility, or some other character flaw. Chemically dependent people were ordered to shape up and get it together, or they were dismissed as "weak-willed" or "just that way."

We know better today. We have substantial evidence that chemical dependence is a disease.

Exactly what causes chemical dependence? The jury is still out on that question, but we do know how to tell if someone has the disease. **That person's relationship with alcohol or other drugs becomes more important that anything else in his or her life.**

Like any other disease, chemical dependence has certain definable characteristics:

1. Chemical dependence is a compulsive and obsessive disease.

For the chemically dependent, using alcohol or other drugs is a compulsion. Compulsion is an irresistible urge to keep repeating the same irrational behavior without the ability to stop. Compulsive drinking or using other drugs is a primary symptom of the disease of chemical dependence. It appears to reside in the old "primitive brain"—technically called the hypothalamic instinctual brain—that houses our strongest instincts: to flee or fight, to eat and drink, to reproduce.

Along with compulsion, there's also an obsession with chemicals. Obsession means a persistent thought or desire to do something or have something, a preoccupation with it. A chemically dependent person is obsessed with such concerns as "Where can I get some?" "How much should I get?" "Where should I hide my supply?" Thoughts about drinking or using dominate this person's thinking and become central to his or her life.

2. Chemical dependence is a primary disease.

A chemically dependent person has a primary relationship with the chemical. This means that it's not just a symptom of some underlying physical, mental, or emotional disorder. Instead, it causes many such disorders. This also means that other problems a chemical dependent may have—such as physical illness, disturbed family relations, depression, unresolved grief issues, and trouble at school or on the job—can't be effectively treated until the person stops using chemicals. The chemical dependence must be treated first.

3. Chemical dependence is a progressive disease.

Once a person enters the addiction process, the disease follows a predictable, progressive course of symptoms. Left untreated, it always gets worse.

The normal progression goes from using chemicals with few consequences to using chemicals with greater and more serious consequences, including physical, mental, emotional, and spiritual deterioration. For example, a chemically dependent person might progress from experiencing a few hangovers, to getting drunk and passing out at a party or family gathering, to getting picked up repeatedly for driving while intoxicated, to losing a job, to becoming physically violent and injuring a friend or family member.

continued on next page

For Your Information . . .

continued

4. Chemical dependence is a chronic disease.

Once a person is addicted to chemicals, the symptoms of the disease become chronic. This means that he or she can never safely use chemicals again. As the saying goes, the alcoholic is always "one drink away from a drunk." There's no cure for this condition. In this respect, chemical dependence is similar to diabetes, another chronic disease. In both cases, the diabetic or chemical dependent can have a healthy, happy, and productive life as long as he or she accepts the need for total abstinence.

It used to be believed that chemical dependence was a "learned" behavior and could be "unlearned." Not true. Even after five, ten, fifteen or more years of sobriety, alcoholics who start drinking again usually begin to drink at the same level at which they left off. It doesn't matter how much intellectual understanding they've acquired about the disease, or how firmly they've resolved to stay off alcohol. Once they take that first drink, they'll take another and another.

Chemical dependence is a lifelong, permanent disease. It never goes away. It can't be cured; it can only be arrested. That's why people who get help and quit using are often called "recovering" and not "recovered."

5. Chemical dependence is a fatal disease.

A chemically dependent person usually dies prematurely if he or she continues to use alcohol or other drugs. The average lifespan of an alcoholic is 10 to 12 years shorter than that of a nonalcoholic. In addition to the medical causes of death that are directly related to chemical dependence, alcoholics are 10 times more likely than alcoholics to die from fires and 6 to 15 times more likely to commit suicide, and drunk driving causes over 50 percent of all highway fatalities.

6. Chemical dependence is a treatable disease.

The five characteristics of chemical dependence just described—compulsive/obsessive, primary, progressive, chronic and fatal—can be discouraging for both the addicted person and others who want to help. But there's a strong, bright light at the end of the tunnel: Chemical dependence can be treated and arrested. Seven out of ten chemically dependent persons who accept treatment and use the knowledge and tools they're given there find sobriety. People can and do both quit using chemicals and get their lives back in order.

Much of the information in this section, The Disease of Chemical Dependence, was adapted from the book *Choices & Consequences: What to Do When a Teenager Uses Alcohol/Drugs* by Dick Schaefer (see Resources section).

45
Signs and Symptoms of Chemical Dependence

GOALS:

- Increase understanding of the various signs and symptoms of chemical dependence
- Encourage students to look for these signs and symptoms in their own chemical use

DESCRIPTION: ▶

Group members choose specific signs and symptoms of chemical dependence from a list and discuss their relevance to their own lives.

DIRECTIONS: ▶

Point out to the group that, just as the common cold has a specific set of symptoms that tell us we've got one, so does chemical dependence have symptoms. Ask group members for a few examples of some of the more common symptoms of chemical dependence, such as getting drunk regularly, dropping out of school, entering a treatment program.

Hand out copies of the list of signs and symptoms (see following page). Pick a student to begin and ask her to choose a symptom from the list, read it out loud, and then choose another group member to respond to the question of whether or not he has experienced this particular symptom. Once he has answered the question, the rest of the group, proceeding in turn around the circle, should also answer this question. The person who first answered the question should continue the discussion by picking another symptom from the list and someone else to begin the discussion. Continue in this fashion for the entire group session.

NOTES: ▶

When you allow students to pick both the question and who will answer, a peculiar thing happens: Group members, aware of each others' drinking and using histories, will choose especially relevant questions and group members to respond. For example, Joe might choose the symptom "hangover or bad trip" and address it first to Shelly because he knows she was hung over last weekend. A certain amount of this somewhat antagonistic dynamic should be allowed, if not subtly encouraged, as it gets to the heart of the matter quickly.

Have enough copies of the signs and symptoms list so that everybody will have a copy to read. When a single list is passed around the circle, time is lost while group members choose from the list.

MATERIALS:

Signs and Symptoms List.

Signs and Symptoms of Chemical Dependence List

1. Increase in the amount of alcohol or other drugs used.
2. Arrested for MIP (Minor in Possession) offense.
3. Dramatic change in mood when drinking or using.
4. Denial of any problem.
5. Dishonesty with peers about drinking or using.
6. Failed attempts to quit or cut down on chemical use.
7. Association with known heavy users.
8. Frequent excuses for chemical use.
9. Protecting supply of chemicals.
10. Low self-image.
11. Hangovers or bad trips.
12. School suspension because of chemical use.
13. Frequent mood changes.
14. Deterioration of school grades.
15. Stealing money for chemicals.
16. Using chemicals while alone.
17. Loss of control while using or drinking.
18. Health problems.
19. Suicidal thoughts or behaviors.
20. Dropped by girlfriend or boyfriend because of chemical use.
21. Violent behavior when high or drunk.
22. Preoccupation with chemicals.
23. Increase in frequency of chemical use.
24. Increase in tolerance.
25. Memory loss.
26. Using chemicals in the morning.
27. Loss of friends.
28. Frequent broken promises.
29. Defensive when confronted.
30. Fired from jobs.

46
The Chemical Curve

GOALS: ▶
- Increase awareness of difference between the levels of use, abuse, and dependence
- Encourage group members to assess their own levels of use

DESCRIPTION: ▶
After a brief presentation concerning the differing levels of use, abuse, and dependence, group members assess their own level of chemical use.

DIRECTIONS: ▶
Begin this session by asking group members to explain what the difference is between someone who does and someone who doesn't have a problem with chemical use. They'll most likely mention obvious differences such as how much and how often a person drinks. Point out to them that there are many other indicators—why a person uses chemicals, or consequences of chemical use, just to name two—and discuss some of these other signs that tell us that someone has a problem with chemical use.

Now ask them if there are really only two categories, "no problem" and "problem." If you ask them "Does everyone who has a problem need to go to a treatment center?" they will no doubt tell you "No." Challenge them to break the "problem" category into separate levels. This will be more difficult for them to do and lends a perfect opportunity for you to make a brief presentation explaining the concept of the levels of use, abuse, and dependence (see following page).

Once this concept is understood, use the remaining time to personalize this information. Ask group members to, one by one, describe their own chemical use in terms of the use, abuse, dependence curve and explain to the group at which level they believe their own chemical use to be.

NOTES: ▶
This also can be an appropriate session to use an assessment questionnaire, especially when the test results will score students on the use, abuse, dependence curve. Administering a questionnaire will require a second session (see activity number 65 for assessment questionnaire information).

MATERIALS: ▶
None required.

For Your Information . . .

Use, Abuse and Dependence

Comparing a person who is abusing chemicals to someone who is dependent upon chemicals is confusing because there can be few discernible differences. Indeed, the chemical abuser might even appear to be using more often or even getting into more trouble than the chemically dependent person. The real difference between the two categories lies in the fact that an abuser still has control over his or her chemical use (whether this person wants to do something about it is a different matter). The dependent person has lost control. This dynamic sheds light on why some young people who are abusing chemicals make changes at some point—they grow up, mellow out, get married, get a job, for example—and still others, looking and acting just like those who abuse chemicals, never seem to break out of the pattern of heavy chemical use and the resultant problems. These people have crossed the line into dependence.

Here are the five different levels of use focusing, in this case, on the drug alcohol. Since teenagers cannot legally drink alcohol, they never fall into the category of "Use" or "Misuse." Their use of alcohol is always considered to be "Abuse."

Here are the five different levels focusing, in this case, on the drug alcohol:

No use - Many people simply don't use mind-altering chemicals. They don't like the taste of alcoholic drinks, they don't like what it does to their bodies, they are minors, it's against their religious teachings.

Use - This category can be defined as using a chemical to enhance an already pleasurable event. Social drinking fits in this category, such as nursing a drink or two at a wedding reception.

Misuse - This category is defined by occasional problems. Someone makes a mistake and gets drunk at a wedding reception even though he or she didn't intend to. Many people learn from these types of experiences and return to the use level.

Abuse - If misuse is occasional problems, abuse is regular problems resulting from the use of chemicals. It's characterized by getting drunk at every wedding reception. Instead of using the consequences of the drunken episode—hung over, embarrassed—as a learning experience and making changes in drinking behavior, a person who abuses chemicals continues to repeat the same mistake over and over again. The chemicals have begun to interfere in this person's life. Still, this person does have control over his or her drinking and can make some changes and move back up into the misuse or the use level if he or she wishes.

Dependence - Once a person becomes dependent on chemicals, he has lost control over his ability to use or not use. The chemicals are now in control. It's no different than a person with the flu saying "I think I will be over this flu by noon today." The flu is in charge. A chemically dependent person would be drunk at the wedding reception despite the promises she made to her husband that she wouldn't drink this time. We can also subdivide this category into early, middle, and late stages, demonstrating that once someone is chemically dependent, there is a downward progression towards what Alcoholics Anonymous refers to as "jails, institutions, and death." Some additional points to consider:

- Teenagers can progress from use to dependence in a matter of 2 or 3 years. The same slide might take a chemically dependent adult 5 to 10 years.

- The longer a person remains at the abuse level, the more likely he or she will cross over into dependence.

- Making a distinction between abuse and dependence in a young person is much more difficult because of other concurrent issues of adolescence.

- Once someone has crossed the line into dependence, he can't return back to responsible use. Whether he is recovering or not, he'll always be chemically dependent.

47
Four Phases of Chemical Dependence

GOALS: ▶
- Create an awareness of the different phases of chemical dependence
- Help students to see chemical dependence as a disease

DESCRIPTION: ▶
The basic concepts of the four phases of chemical dependence is illustrated through the use of a brief lecture combined with demonstration and discussion.

DIRECTIONS: ▶
Begin this session by pointing out to the group that chemical dependence isn't something that happens overnight—it's a process with four different stages. And, in order to better understand what chemical dependence is, it's helpful to understand what these stages are.

First ask group members to explain the progression of chemical dependence in their own words. Once the group has struggled with this briefly, come to their rescue with a brief presentation using the information on the following page. In order to make this information more meaningful, use the group to demonstrate the four stages as you explain them. Begin by asking two students to sit in the center of the group circle. These two students will represent chemicals (let them choose which chemical). Also choose one student to "contract" chemical dependence. The remaining circle of students will represent life.

As you explain the first phase (learning), ask the chemically dependent student to enter the circle and briefly join the two students representing chemicals. He should make a return visit to the chemicals as you explain the second stage (seeking). During the explanation of the third stage (loss of choice), he should return to the chemicals again, but the students representing the chemicals should grab him tight and only let him go after he promises to return later. Then, during the explanation of the fourth and final stage (using to feel normal), he should be grabbed by the chemicals and not let go.

After this demonstration, use the remaining time to discuss which phase group members think they are in. As group members take turns telling the group which level they fit in, ask them questions that require them to explain their answer in more detail.

NOTES: ▶
In order to make the demonstration more effective, you might consider taking the two group members who will be representing the chemicals aside and explaining their roles to them privately, rather than in front of the rest of the group.Also be sure to mention that many people do recover from chemical dependence. Many people who were in the fourth stage are now leading happy, sober lives.

QUESTIONS: ▶
- Why do you think that you are in this phase?
- How long have you been in this phase?
- Do you think that you will move into the next phase? Why or why not?
- Do you know anyone who is in the third or fourth phase?

MATERIALS: ▶
None required.

For Your Information. . .

The Four Phases of Chemical Dependence

Phase one: Learning: As people first use a chemical, such as alcohol, they learn that this chemical changes how they are feeling, usually in a positive way. This is a pleasant experience for most people, and, once the effects of the chemical wear off, they return to normal.

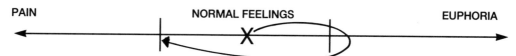

Phase two: Seeking: After several experiences with the chemical, people move out of the learning stage and into the seeking stage. A person in this stage knows what alcohol will do and she knows how much she needs to drink in order to get this certain effect. Unfortunately, some people in this stage use these mind-altering chemicals in an attempt to get rid of uncomfortable feelings, such as anger or loneliness. This is a temporary solution, however, because the painful feelings return—unsolved—when the effects of the chemical have worn off.

Phase three: Loss of Choice: Some people move from the second stage into the third stage. This stage signals the presence of chemical dependence. People in this stage have lost the ability to choose whether to use chemicals or not. Up until this stage a person could choose from many different ways to deal with his feelings, but now he relies on only one way—the use of chemicals. Whenever he is feeling bad, he turns to the chemicals for relief. So the chemicals are now in control. We still don't completely understand why some people move from the second to the third stage and other people stay in the first or second stage.

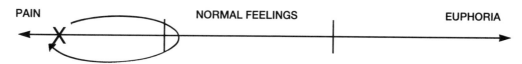

Stage four: Using to Feel Normal: This last stage is a dangerous place characterized by deterioration in all areas of life—loss of job, failing health, suicide. A person in this stage is always feeling bad and uses chemicals in an attempt just to feel normal once again. When a person reaches this stage of chemical dependence, most everyone recognizes that there is a problem. It would be hard not to.

48
Research Report

GOALS: ▶
- Increase understanding of chemical dependence
- Eliminate common misconceptions about chemical dependence

DESCRIPTION: ▶
Students are each assigned a topic word to research. The following week of group each student gives a small report to the group about what she has learned.

DIRECTIONS: ▶
From the list of vocabulary words (see following page), ask each student to select a term. Ask them to research this word in the library or to use other resources such as a discussion with a recovering person or counselor. The following week of group, ask each student to spend a few minutes explaining this key term to the rest of the group. If they are able, ask the group member to relate a personal example that connects this term to her personal life. For example, if the term were "tolerance," the student could explain what tolerance is and then also describe how she has noticed that it takes her twice as many beers to get drunk now as compared to when she first started drinking. Encourage the rest of the group to ask questions of the person who is explaining the term.

MATERIALS: ▶
Chemical Dependence Terms.

Chemical Dependence Terms

aftercare
Al-Anon
Alateen
Alcoholics Anonymous
Big Book
blackouts
chemical dependence
co-dependence
congruence
defenses
delirium tremens
delusion
detach
disengage
dry drunk
dysfunctional
enabling
family disease
halfway house
hitting bottom
intervention
letting go
leveling
minimizing
Narcotics Anonymous
nurturing
physical addiction
psychological addiction
rationalizing
recovery
recovery program
relapse
reverse tolerance
therapy
tolerance
treatment center
Twelve Steps

49
Book Report

GOALS: ▶
- Increase awareness of available media resources
- Learn more about chemical dependence

DESCRIPTION: ▶
Group members choose a book or video from the selection the group leader has brought to group. The following week, students give a brief report to the rest of the group.

DIRECTIONS: ▶
Bring a number of print and video resources to group. These resources should include books, workbooks, and videos that are both age- and topic-appropriate for the group members (see Resources section).

Ask the students to select one book or video each and be prepared to give a short report to the rest of the group. These reports should be informal verbal reports about what the student learned from the book or video. Use the next session of group for the students' reports.

QUESTIONS: ▶
- What did you learn by reading the book or watching the video?
- What are three important points that the book or video is making?
- Would you recommend this book or video to other students? Why or why not?

NOTES: ▶
Be sensitive to the fact that some students might be uncomfortable viewing the tape at home or might not have access to a VCR. When this is the case, arrange access to a VCR at school that students could use after school or during a study hall period.

MATERIALS: ▶
Selection of books, workbooks, pamphlets, and videos.

50
Chemical Dependence
Crosswords

GOALS:

- Increase students' chemical dependence vocabulary
- Encourage teamwork and group unity

DESCRIPTION:

Opposing teams work to complete a crossword puzzle composed of chemical dependence terms

DIRECTIONS:

Split the support group into equal teams. Ask each team to choose a captain. The captain is responsible for communicating the team's answers and question choices to the leader. The support group leader shouldn't accept any answers from team members other than the team captain. Draw the empty frame of the puzzle on the blackboard and choose which team will go first. Each team gets thirty seconds for their turn regardless of how many blanks they fill. When it is a team's turn they choose a horizontal or vertical blank line. The leader then reads the clue for this blank out loud. The team should discuss possible answers among themselves before the team captain offers the answer to the leader. If the team is correct, it receives one point and may continue with a new clue, providing there still is time remaining on the thirty-second clock. The support group leader should write correct definitions in the puzzle squares as they are identified. If their answer is incorrect, they must move on to a new crossword clue (they can return to this clue next turn if they wish). When thirty seconds have passed, their turn is finished and the next team begins. The game continues until all clues have been answered.

NOTES:

Two crossword puzzles representing different levels of difficulty are provided (see following page) so that you may pick a puzzle with age-appropriate vocabulary.

If you require additional puzzles, either design them yourself or, if you have at least two different support groups, ask the groups to design and then swap puzzles.

MATERIALS:

Crossword puzzles, thirty-second timer or clock, blackboard.

Puzzle A
ACROSS 3) defenses 4) blackout 8) pills 10) feelings 11) bottles 12) Alateen 14) anger 15) listen 17) sad 20) abuse 21) adults. **DOWN** 1) help 2) alcoholic 3) drugs 5) chemicals 6) treatment 7) disease 9) steps 13) talk 16) stress 18) drunk 19) group
Puzzle B
ACROSS 2) chemical 3) ACOA 6) defenses 7) narcotics 8) book 11) control 12) Step 14) treatment 16) anger 18) enable 19) Alateen 21) relapse 23) nurturing 24) Twelve 25) dry drunk 26) blackout **DOWN** 1) halfway 2) CA 4) addiction 5) recovering 6) dysfunctional 9) Anonymous 10) confront 11) codependence 13) aftercare 15) tolerance 17) intervention 20) family 22) drunk 23) new

Crossword Puzzle A

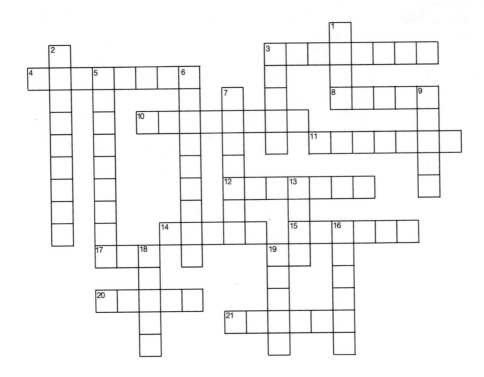

ACROSS

3 We protect ourselves with these

4 Alcohol-induced memory loss

8 Sleeping _____

10 It's important to talk about these

11 Sometimes we want to throw these out

12 Where young people can get help

14 Rage

15 How friends can help

17 Feeling blue

20 Physical or verbal

21 When in danger, reach out to _____

DOWN

1 A cry for _____

2 Addicted to C2H5OH

3 Substances that can change your feelings

5 Pills, marijuana, alcohol

6 Where alcoholics and addicts go for help

7 Alcoholism is a _____

9 The Twelve _____

13 The secret for feeling better

16 Tension and anxiety

18 Intoxicated

19 Support _____

Crossword Puzzle B

ACROSS

2 _____ dependence
3 Adults who have an alcoholic parent
6 Used to protect ourselves
7 Heroin, opium
8 The Big _____ of Alcoholics Anonymous
11 A symptom of drinking problems is lack of _____
12 The First _____
14 Where chemically dependent people go for help
16 Rage
18 Allow the problem to continue
19 Al-Anon for young people
21 Return to using chemicals
23 Supporting and encouraging
24 _____ Steps
25 Not recovering but not drinking (2 words)
26 Alcohol-induced memory loss

DOWN

1 _____ house
2 Cocaine Anonymous
4 Can be physical or psychological
5 Clean and sober
6 Not working well
9 Alcoholics _____
10 Present reality
11 The illness of family members
13 After treatment
15 Need more chemicals because of increased _____
17 Formal group confrontation
20 _____disease
22 Intoxicated
23 Sobriety provides a _____ outlook

51
Blood-Alcohol Content

Stage: 2-3

Challenge: LOW

Grades: 9-12

GOALS: ▶
- Emphasize the dangers of drinking and driving
- Teach students how to assess their degree of impairment when they've been drinking

DESCRIPTION: ▶ Students learn about blood-alcohol content (BAC) and estimate their own BAC for various amounts of ingested alcohol.

DIRECTIONS: ▶ Begin this session by asking group members to share some examples of car crashes they are aware of that involved alcohol. Usually everybody is aware of at least one major crash in which a student or someone else they knew was injured or killed because of drinking and driving.

Once the serious nature of this problem is evident, make a brief presentation that explains how alcohol affects a person's ability to drive and how blood-alcohol level is determined (see **For Your Information** on page 112). After this material is presented, hand out copies of the blood-alcohol content worksheet (see following pages) and allow group members time to complete it. Spend the remaining time discussing what they've learned about their own BAC levels and their own experiences with drinking and driving.

QUESTIONS: ▶
- Do any of you know someone who's been injured or killed because of drinking and driving? What happened?
- Have you ever been in a car with someone driving who's been drunk? How did that feel?
- Have you ever driven a car while alcohol-impaired?
- Will you drive a car while alcohol-impaired in the future?
- How will you make sure that this doesn't happen?

MATERIALS: ▶ **Blood-Alcohol Content** worksheet.

Blood-Alcohol Content Worksheet

BLOOD ALCOHOL CHART

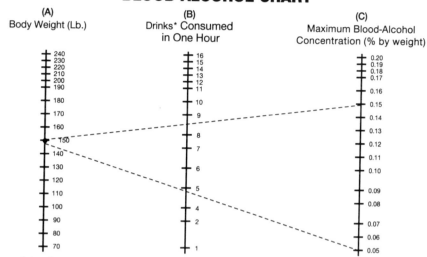

(A) Body Weight (Lb.)	(B) Drinks* Consumed in One Hour	(C) Maximum Blood-Alcohol Concentration (% by weight)

To use this chart:

First Locate your weight in column A.

Second Locate in column B the number of drinks* you drank in one hour.

Third Draw a straight line from column A to B and continue over to column C. This third column will show your estimated blood alcohol content.

* For this chart, one drink is a 12-oz can of beer, a 4-oz glass of wine, or one ounce of eighty-proof liquor (straight or in a mixed drink.) Larger drinks, or a mixed drink with more than one ounce of eighty-proof liquor, may qualify as two or even more drinks.

Use the chart above to answer these questions:

1 What was your BAC during your last drinking experience?

2 Figure your BAC for the following quantities of alcohol consumed in one hour:

2 beers	BAC = _____
3 mixed drinks	BAC = _____
4 glasses of wine	BAC = _____
5 beers	BAC = _____
4 beers and 2 mixed drinks	BAC = _____
3 straight shots and 4 beers	BAC = _____

For Your Information . . .

Blood-Alcohol Content

Ethyl alcohol, the type of alcohol used in beverages, is a mind altering-chemical that acts as a general depressant on the brain and the nervous system. The first areas of the brain that are affected by ethyl alcohol are memory, reasoning, as well as reaction time and coordination. These last two areas are factors crucial to driving an automobile. It shouldn't be surprising that 50 percent of traffic fatalities involve drunk driving and that alcohol-related traffic fatalities are the leading cause of death among 15- to 24-year-olds.

It makes no difference whether a person is drinking wine, whiskey, or beer. They all contain the same chemical, alcohol, and in roughly the same amounts since one can of beer, one mixed drink, and one glass of wine all contain roughly one ounce of alcohol.

Alcohol doesn't require digestion to begin its affects. It is absorbed immediately into the bloodstream through the walls of the stomach and the small intestine. The rate of absorption is affected somewhat by factors such as the presence of food in the stomach. After absorption, the alcohol circulates throughout the bloodstream, reaching and directly impacting brain functioning. Alcohol is removed from the bloodstream mostly through the process of oxidization, which takes place in the liver. The liver needs about one hour to oxidize each ounce of alcohol. Contrary to popular wisdom, nothing can speed up this process. Not cold showers, exercising, or coffee.

Blood-alcohol content (BAC) is expressed as a percentage of the amount of alcohol in a person's blood. Three factors affect this percentage: number of drinks consumed, time frame, and body weight. Of course, the amount of alcohol consumed affects one's BAC but so does the time frame, because three drinks in as many hours will result in a very low BAC while three drinks in one hour will result in a much higher BAC. A person's body weight is the third piece to this equation: 3 drinks in one hour consumed by a 170 = pound person will result in a BAC of roughly .05%, while 3 drinks in an hour consumed by someone only 100 lbs. will result in a BAC of .09%.

Affects of Blood Alcohol Content

0.02 - .03% Reaction time is slowed; behavior less controlled.

0.05% Loss of coordination and driving skill. Increased likelihood of an auto accident.

0.08 - 0.10% Legally impaired in most states. Noticeable effects on judgment and coordination. Six times more likely to have an auto accident.

0.15 - 0.20 Seriously effects on vision, coordination, and judgment. A person is 25 to 50 times more likely to have an auto accident.

Section E: Self-assessment

This section of activities represents the core curriculum of a typical support group for students in trouble with their own chemical use. Paging through this section you'll note that the activities and worksheets have a common theme of examining various aspects of chemical use. It's not that group members don't really know how much marijuana they're smoking or beer they're drinking—it's that denial makes the picture cloudy. The activities help to present reality to group members in a slightly different fashion over and over again: here is how much crystal you're using, here is how often you do it, here is the trouble it's causing you. Like a carnival house of mirrors, wherever group members turn, they continue to be presented with the painful truth: your chemical use is a problem.

As can be imagined, this isn't a pleasant process. Group members won't like what they see. Expect resistance. And when the going gets rough, remind yourself that the fact group members are troubled by an activity is actually a good sign—it means that you, the activity, and the group are getting through to them. Uncomfortable as this may be (sometimes for you as well as them), it's really why they are in the group in the first place.

52
Chemical Matrix

GOALS: ▶
- Make an assessment concerning students' chemical use
- Increase students' awareness of their own chemical use

DESCRIPTION: ▶
Group members record their chemical use during the previous week and discuss the implication in group.

DIRECTIONS: ▶
At the beginning of each group session, hand out the **Chemical Matrix** worksheet (see following page) so that group members can record their previous week's chemical use. You may wish to discuss their previous week's use at the beginning of every group session for a few minutes, or set aside time for this discussion during, say, the fourth group session and then the final group session. Regardless of your approach, collect the worksheets every week. Giving students their worksheets so that they can record their chemical use as their week progresses usually results in the worksheets getting misplaced.

QUESTIONS: ▶
- Is this past week's usage more, less, or a typical amount of chemical use for you?
- Do you feel comfortable with this pattern of use, or would you like it to be less?
- Looking over previous weeks of the matrix, what patterns do you see?
- What patterns of chemical use would you like to see on your matrix?

NOTES: ▶
Often, students will complain that they can't remember their past week's chemical use exactly. Tell them that they should just do their best and to estimate if they can't remember the exact amount.

MATERIALS: ▶
Chemical Matrix worksheet.

Chemical Matrix Worksheet

Write today's day in the first blank and fill in the rest of the blanks consecutively. For example, if today is Wednesday, then write Wednesday, Thursday, Friday, and so on. Now record your chemical use in the boxes for the previous week. The first box should contain your chemical use for a week ago today and the last box will contain your chemical use for yesterday. Fill in both the type of chemicals and the amount—5 beers, or 1 joint, for example.

Days of the Week

One week ago today →

Yesterday ←

Week 1

Week 1

Week 1

Week 1

Week 1

Week 1

Week 7

53
Abstinence Contracts

GOALS: ▶
- Encourage students to abstain from chemicals
- Provide constructive consequences for chemical use

DESCRIPTION: ▶
Group members sign abstinence contracts containing consequences that address their specific situations and needs.

DIRECTIONS: ▶
Discuss with group members the importance of their chemical abstinence for the duration of the support group cycle. Their participation in this group is a time for them to learn about themselves, their feelings, their problems, and the true extent of the nature of their own chemical abuse. This will be difficult to do if they are busy drinking or getting high during the weeks that they are in the group. Challenge them to make a commitment to stay abstinent for the duration of the group cycle. Stress that this abstinence includes all mind-altering chemicals, including alcohol (the exception would be drugs prescribed by a physician). This should be formalized by a written contract (see following page). Ask them to read over the contract and fill in the appropriate blanks. They should do this individually, not as a group, since negative group pressure can easily influence the contents of the contract. Once everyone has completed a contract, collect them and ask group members to tell the group what sort of commitment they made and whether they think this will be an easy or difficult commitment to keep.

NOTES: ▶
These contracts can assist students in abstaining from chemicals, but they can also create dishonesty and secrecy in group when someone breaks his contract and is afraid to talk about it. For this reason, it's best not to put undo pressure on group members to make a pledge that they have no intention of keeping. If a group member isn't willing to make an abstinence pledge, then ask him what he is willing to commit to. Perhaps he is willing to cut his chemical use by half, or quit smoking pot. For someone who is chemically dependent, these halfway measures are generally nonproductive except for the fact that if this student makes a sincere commitment—whatever that commitment may be—and isn't able to keep it, then that broken commitment is one more indication that this person has a problem.

Some members of the group are participating because of specific consequences that brought them to this group. These students are most likely—and should be if they aren't—already on a no-use contract. This within-the-group contract should reflect their outside obligations such as going in for a chemical evaluation if they use again.

MATERIALS: ▶
Abstinence Contract.

Abstinence Contract

I will not use any mind-altering chemicals for the following time period:

_____ through _____ .

If I were to break that commitment, I will take these steps:

1 _____

2. _____

3. _____

These would be my consequences:

1. _____

2. _____

3. _____

Signed _____ Date _____

Witnessed_____

54
My Day by the Slice

GOALS: ▶

- Assess amount of time devoted to chemical use
- Encourage students to review how they use their time

DESCRIPTION: ▶

Students complete a worksheet that details how they spend their time.

DIRECTIONS: ▶

Begin this session by asking group members for examples of activities they usually do during the day. Encourage them to list as many as they can think of, from sleeping to watching TV, from eating to driving around, from getting high to doing homework. You may wish to ask them to make a list of these activities on the blackboard that they can refer to during the second part of this activity.

    Pass out the **Time Wheel** worksheet (see following page) and crayons or colored pencils. When everyone has finished, ask them to give their worksheet to the person on their right. Now that everyone has a different group member's worksheet, spend the time remaining in this session discussing their answers.

QUESTIONS: ▶

- What conclusions can you draw after looking at your neighbor's **Time Wheel**? What does she spend the most time doing? The least?
- What percentage of the **Time Wheel** does using chemicals or doing chemical-related activities occupy?
- Would you like the amount of time spent using chemicals you outlined on your Time Wheel to change?

MATERIALS: ▶

Time Wheel worksheet, crayons or colored pencils.

Time Wheel

Write activities typical to a day in your life in an area of the wheel. Make the size of the sections represent how much time is spent for each particular activity. Color each area a different color. For example, if you generally sleep eight hours, then color a third of the circle blue and label it "sleeping."

55
My Relationship with Chemicals

GOALS: ▶
- Encourage self-assessment of group members' relationship with chemicals
- Demonstrate how students' relationships with chemicals interfere with other relationships

DESCRIPTION: ▶

Group members draw a diagram that demonstrates their relationship with chemicals, people, activities, and things. These drawings are interpreted and discussed by the group.

DIRECTIONS: ▶

Give each student a sheet of newsprint and a marker. Ask them to write their names in the center of the page and to draw a circle around it. Once done, ask them to write words that describe chemicals they use, people with whom they have relationships, activities that are important to them, and things that are important to them on the paper, putting a circle around each one.

Once their pages are filled with these circles, ask them to draw connecting lines radiating out from their name in the center to the various circles. In addition, they should signify the importance of this relationship by making the line single, double, or triple (see following page for an example.) After the students have finished these drawings, spend the rest of the session discussing their drawings. One effective approach to this discussion is to ask a student to hold up her drawing for the rest of the group to see, and then to ask the group to interpret and describe this particular student's relationships.

QUESTIONS: ▶
- Which relationships are the most important to you?
- Which relationships are insignificant to you?
- Would you like to change the status of some of these relationships? Which ones?
- How would you makes these changes?
- What has changed about your relationships since you've begun using chemicals?
- Does your chemical use interfere with any of your other relationships?

MATERIALS: ▶

Newsprint and markers.

My Relationship with Chemicals Example

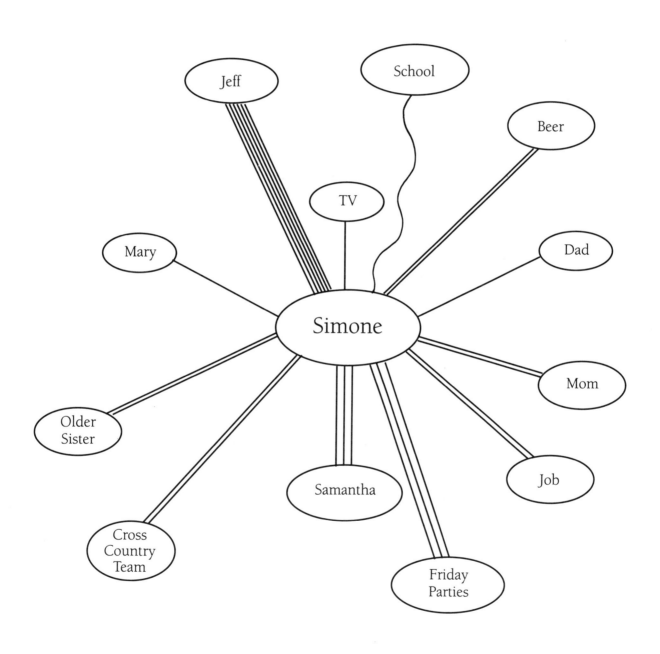

56
Chemicals and Growing Up

Stage: 2-3

Challenge: HIGH

Grades: 9-12

GOALS:

- Assess how chemical use has interfered with growth processes
- Identify areas that need improvement

DESCRIPTION: ▶

Students complete a worksheet that helps them examine how their chemical use has interfered with fundamental tasks of adolescence.

DIRECTIONS: ▶

Introduce this session by asking the group to name some of the lessons that they must learn while growing up through adolescence. Typical examples include how to get a job, dating, taking care of themselves, figuring out who they are. Then ask them to identify things that can interfere with learning these important lessons, such as emotional problems, chemical dependence, dropping out of school. Ask them for examples of how these things can interfere. Spend some time focusing on how chemical dependence can interfere with learning these life skills by again asking for specific examples.

Hand out copies of the **Chemicals and Growing Up** worksheet (see following page). When all have completed it, spend the remainder of the session discussing their answers.

MATERIALS:

Chemicals and Growing Up worksheet.

Chemicals and Growing Up

Adolescence is a time when important personal changes take place and many important lessons must be learned. If you are busy using chemicals during this time, some of this emotional growth is interfered with and may not take place at all. How has your chemical use affected you from accomplishing each of the following growing-up goals? Examples are provided to help you understand each category.

Developing an identity: (I only see myself as a burnout. I used to be great in sports, but now I'm known as a partier.)

Gaining independence: (My folks don't trust me at all since they found dope in my room. I can't get a job because of my long hair.)

Making friends: (My reputation is a stoner. I don't have many friends unless I've got a new bag of pot.)

Planning for the future: (My grades aren't good enough to get into college. Last summer I just partied all the time instead of looking for a job.)

What other growing-up goals do you need to work on? Why?

The above material has been adapted from *Can I Handle Alcohol/ Drugs?* by David Zarek and James Sipe (see Resources section).

57A
The Chemicals I Use

GOALS: ▶
- Help students understand why they use specific chemicals
- Assess the number of chemicals a student uses

DESCRIPTION: ▶ Students complete a worksheet that helps them look at what chemicals they use and why. Their answers are discussed in the group.

DIRECTIONS: ▶ Hand out **The Chemicals I Use** worksheet (see following page) for group members to complete. When they are finished, spend the rest of the session discussing their answers.

QUESTIONS: ▶
- Why do you prefer using some chemicals over others?
- What problems does using your chosen chemical present for you?
- What are the dangers associated with the chemicals you use?
- Has your chemical preference changed over the past several years? Why?
- What was your preferred chemical in the past?

NOTES: ▶ This activity and the next, **My Chemical History**, are so closely related that I have named them 57A and 57B. It is not necessary to do them in that order, and each exercise does stand alone.

MATERIALS: ▶ **The Chemicals I Use** worksheet.

The Chemicals I Use

List the chemicals you've used, starting with the chemical you use the most at the top and finishing with the chemical you use the least at the bottom. Then fill in your reasons for using each chemical in the righthand column, such as liking the feeling it gives me, sleeping better, it gets me fired up and rowdy. Finish this worksheet by writing a 1, 2, and a 3 by your three favorite chemicals.

Chemical name	**Reasons for using this chemical**

57B
My Chemical History

GOALS: ▶
- Have students assess their chemical use
- Become aware of the risks of chemical use
- Familiarize group leaders with students' chemical use

DESCRIPTION: ▶
Group members complete a worksheet that details their experiences with mind-altering chemicals. This information is then discussed in group.

DIRECTIONS: ▶
Explain to the group that it can be informative for them to take a look at their own personal history of chemical use—what chemicals they've used, when they started, and how often they use them. Pass out the **Chemical History** worksheet for everyone to complete. Encourage them to be specific in their answers. When completed correctly, the worksheets will not only indicate which chemicals they've used and when they started, but will also describe how both quantity and frequency has changed over time. This trend information is important because it will show how their use of particular chemicals has progressed from infrequently to regularly—from experimentation to a problem. When they have completed the worksheets, spend the remainder of the session discussing their answers. Be sure to share your impressions of a student's chemical history—noting variety of chemicals used, amount of use, and any trends reflecting an increase in use—after she shares her worksheet.

MATERIALS: ▶
Chemical History worksheet.

Chemical History

Name_____ Date_____

This worksheet is a summary of your experiences with mind-altering chemicals—how much and how often, both past and present. Under the Past category, write in how old you were when you first used that chemical, and then how much and how often during the first year. Under the Present category, write in how much and how often you currently use that chemical. Do this for every chemical you have used on the list.

(The first line is filled in as example.)

	Age	Amount	Frequency	Amount	Frequency
Alcohol	13	3 beers	once a week	6 beers	twice a week
Alcohol (beer, wine, liquor)					
Marijuana (pot, hash, hash oil)					
Uppers (speed, crystal, crosstops)					
Downers (ludes, barbs, tranquilizers)					
Hallucinogens (LSD, acid, mushrooms)					
Inhalants (glue, gasoline, rush)					
Codeine (in cough syrup or in pain medication)					
Heroin (smack)					
Cocaine (snow, crack)					
PCP (angel dust)					
Other (specify)					

58
Chemicals and Recreation

GOALS: ▶
- Assess how chemicals have interfered with students recreational pursuits
- Identify nonchemical recreation that students can pursue

DESCRIPTION: ▶

Students complete a worksheet that assesses how their chemical use has interfered with their recreational pursuits. Students also identify examples of recreation they can pursue that don't involve chemical use.

DIRECTIONS: ▶

Ask group members to make a list on the blackboard of the things they used to do for fun when they were younger and didn't use chemicals, such as baseball, riding bikes, talking with friends, night games. Encourage them to make this list as extensive as possible.

Then ask them to make another list beside this one of all the activities they typically do for fun now that don't involve chemicals. Most likely this new list will be dramatically shorter. Challenge them to explain this difference. Point out to them that people often begin using chemicals to enhance an already pleasurable event: it makes the party more exciting, it makes listening to the music more enjoyable, it makes the date more relaxing. But, as the chemicals become more and more important to people who use them regularly, eventually the chemicals become the focus, not the party, music, or date. And, when people become really hooked into the chemicals, they forget about recreational activities altogether and concentrate on drinking or getting high.

Hand out the **Chemicals and Recreation** worksheet (see following page). After they have finished, spend the remaining time discussing their answers.

MATERIALS: ▶

Chemicals and Recreation worksheet.

Chemicals and Recreation

Name_____ Date_____

How old were you when you started using chemicals regularly? _____

List all of the recreational activities you enjoyed before this age in the **Before** column.

	Before	**Now?**	**Why not?**
1	_____	_____	_____
2	_____	_____	_____
3	_____	_____	_____
4	_____	_____	_____
5	_____	_____	_____
6	_____	_____	_____
7	_____	_____	_____
8	_____	_____	_____

Next, complete the **Now** column by looking back over your list of activities and answering the question, Do you still do this activity *regularly*? Write in a yes or a no in this column. Now finish the worksheet by thinking about the question, Why don't you do this activity any longer? and writing the answer in the **Why not?** column.

List all activities you do for fun now:

1   6

2   7

3   8

4   9

5   10

Go back over this last list and draw a line through all of the activities that involve chemicals.

59
Friendship Maps

GOALS:

- Assess relationship between students' chemical use and their peers
- Understand the impact of peer pressure
- Discuss the difference between positive and negative friends

DESCRIPTION: ▶

Students describe the quantity and type of friends that they associate with, and discuss how this affects their chemical use.

DIRECTIONS: ▶

Explain to the students how friendships are two-way streets: their friends affect them and the decisions they make, but they also choose friends that are "of the same mind."

Hand out sheets of newsprint to all group members and ask everyone to write their name in the center and draw a circle around it. Next, they should write names and draw circles around them for all of the friends they've had in the past five years, including current and former friends.

Once their sheets are full of circled names, ask them to draw connecting lines from their own circle out to their friend circles. They should connect their own circle with their friend's circles by drawing from one to three lines, signifying the closeness of the relationship. If a particular name on their sheet is a former friend, they could show this with a zigzag or broken line. Once you have given them a few minutes to do this, ask them to use a different color marker and draw the outline of a joint or a beer can over the friends with whom they use chemicals. These friendship maps (see example on the following page) will demonstrate a group member's pattern of friends as well as how many of these relationships involve chemicals.

MATERIALS:

Newsprint and markers.

Friendship Map

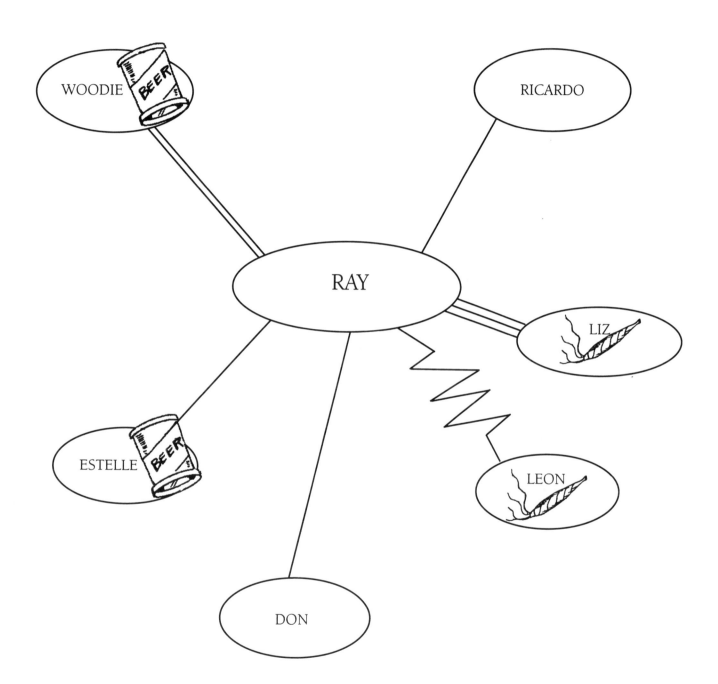

60
Chemicals and Behaviors

GOALS:

- Assess how students' chemical use has affected their behavior
- Identify patterns of chemical use-related behavior

DESCRIPTION:

Students use a worksheet and discussion to examine how their own chemical use has affected their behavior patterns.

DIRECTIONS:

Using the blackboard, ask group members to list behaviors that indicate when people are in trouble with their chemical use. Typical answers include protecting their supply, stealing alcohol or other drugs, passing out, being drunk all the time, getting defensive.

Discuss with the group how it is typical for students' behavior patterns to start changing as they develop a relationship with chemicals. They spend more time finding ways to get high, they start avoiding their family and other personally significant adults, they change peer groups.

Pass out the **Chemicals and Behaviors** worksheet (see following page). Encourage students to think about the questions and to answer them honestly. Spend the rest of the session discussing their answers.

MATERIALS:

Chemicals and Behaviors worksheet.

Chemicals and Behaviors

As people spend more and more time using chemicals, their behaviors start to revolve around these chemicals. Think carefully about these questions before you answer.

Getting the chemicals: spending all your money, borrowing or stealing from others to purchase chemicals, going into risky situations, spending all your time at parties.

What are some things you do to get chemicals?

Using behaviors: getting loud, rude, silly, quiet, or picking fights when you are under the influence of chemicals.

What are you like when you are using chemicals?

Making amends behaviors: apologizing to friends, being dishonest to parents, making excuses to teachers because of the things you've done while you were using chemicals.

What are some ways you've had to make amends for your chemical use?

The above material has been adapted from *Can I Handle Alcohol/ Drugs?* by David Zarek and James Sipe (see Resources section).

61
Chemicals and Feelings

Stage: 2-3
Challenge: MODERATE
Grades: ALL

GOALS: ▶
- Identify relationship between chemical use and feelings
- Encourage students to understand their feelings

DESCRIPTION: ▶
Students focus on feelings and their relationship to chemical use by completing a worksheet that addresses this issue.

DIRECTIONS: ▶
Ask the group this question: "Why do people use chemicals?" Write their answer on the blackboard, answers that will most likely include being cool, peer pressure, having a good time, the taste. Make sure to point out, if nobody does, that one of the fundamental reasons that people use chemicals is to change how they are currently feeling.

Now ask them for examples of some of the feelings that people might want to change. Typical examples include going out drinking when angry, getting high and mellowing out when frustrated. Hand out the **Chemicals and Feelings** worksheet for group members to complete (see following page). When they're finished, ask them to share their answers with the rest of the group.

MATERIALS: ▶
Chemicals and Feelings worksheet.

Chemicals and Feelings

People often use chemicals to change how they are feeling—after all, nobody likes to feel angry, frustrated, lonely, sad. Circle all the feelings that you've tried to change by using chemicals.

afraid	frightened	hostile	lonely	sad
angry	frustrated	hurt	miserable	troubled
anxious	furious	inadequate	nervous	tense
bored	guilty	insecure	paranoid	troubled
confused	hopeless	jealous	rejected	unloved

Now, for each of the feelings that you've tried to change with chemicals, describe an example from your own life (what chemical, in what setting, what happened).

Feeling   **How I tried to change the feeling and what happened**

_____ _____

_____ _____

_____ _____

_____ _____

_____ _____

_____ _____

_____ _____

_____ _____

_____ _____

_____ _____

62
Chemicals and Defenses

GOALS: ▶
- Help students understand the nature of defenses
- Encourage students to identify their own defenses

DESCRIPTION: ▶

Group members are taught the difference between healthy and unhealthy defenses and through both worksheet and discussion identify which defenses they use.

DIRECTIONS: ▶

Ask group members to describe what defenses are. Ask them if they think defenses are healthy or unhealthy. If they are struggling with this question, point out to the group that sometimes defenses are appropriate but that other times they can be a problem. Using the **For Your Information** section on page 138, make a brief presentation to the group concerning the difference between healthy and unhealthy defenses.

Ask group members for examples of defenses that people in trouble with chemicals use, such as minimizing, dishonesty, or anger. List these on the blackboard. They might not be able to name the defense, but encourage them to describe it and give an example. Make sure that everyone understands the four defenses listed on the worksheet (see following page), asking them for examples of each one. Hand out the worksheet and when they're finished, discuss their answers.

MATERIALS: ▶

Chemicals and Defenses worksheet.

Chemicals and Defenses

Here are some common defenses from people who use chemicals. Give three examples of a time when you have used each of these four defenses.

Denying: refusing to accept the way things really are.

1.

2.

3.

Rationalizing: making excuses so that everything seems okay.

1.

2.

3.

Blaming: trying to make other people or places responsible.

1.

2.

3.

Minimizing: making something look less serious than it really is.

1.

2.

3.

What are some other defenses that you have used? Give an example for each defense that you list.

Defense	Example
1. _____	_____
2. _____	_____
3. _____	_____
4. _____	_____
5. _____	_____

For Your Information . . .

Defenses

People naturally develop defenses to protect themselves from threatening or uncomfortable thoughts, feeling, or situations. This is a normal process that helps them cope with fear, frustration, anxiety, and conflict.

We use defenses to *deny* or "change" reality to prevent ourselves from becoming aware of painful thoughts, to avoid painful feelings, to escape situations that are threatening (or seem to be), and to protect ourselves from facing the unpleasant consequences of our own behavior. For example:

Dawne occasionally baby-sat her younger brother. One day Dawne's boyfriend came over to take her for a ride in his new car. Although Dawne knew she shouldn't leave her brother at home alone, she rationalized leaving by telling herself, "I'll only be gone a little while. Besides, he's taking a nap and won't even know I'm gone." While Dawne was away her mother came home unexpectedly.

When Dawne returned, her mother was furious and confronted Dawne about her irresponsible behavior. Then Dawne realized what she'd done, felt guilty, admitted her mistake, and promised it would never happen again.

Dawne first used a defense, *rationalization*, to convince herself that it was okay to take a ride with her boyfriend. But when her mother confronted her with the reality of the situation, Dawne chose to accept reality (and to experience her feelings) rather than to continue rationalizing her wrongdoing. This is an example of a *normal defense*—a defense that the normal person wisely abandons when confronted. with the real situation.

Normal defenses change the way we see a situation in order to make it easier to deal with. However, we are still able to let in enough outside information about the real situation to adjust our thinking, as Dawne did when she was confronted.

Steady chemical users, though, often become less able to accept painful reality, especially when confronted with the harmful consequences of their chemical use. This is partly because of the powerful "masking effects" of chemicals on feelings that cause a person to lose touch with the real situation. It also happens because as time goes on, steady chemical users' defenses become stronger and more rigid and therefore block out the insight they need if they're to change. For example:

Kevin was driving home from a party when he was stopped by the police because of his loud muffler. The officer smelled alcohol and gave him a breath test, which he failed. He was arrested and jailed overnight, was later found guilty, had to pay a fine, and had his license taken away.

Kevin felt no remorse and accepted no responsibility for his actions. He *minimized* the seriousness of the offense, denied having had more than three beers that night, and blamed his conviction on the "stupid cops who've got nothing better to do than hassle people." This is an example of using rigid or *harmful defenses*. In this case, harmful defenses protected Kevin so completely that he filtered out all the painful information. As a result, he was blind to his situation and unable to change his behavior or to make amends.

The above material has been adapted from *Can I Handle Alcohol / Drugs?* by David Zerek and James Sipe (see Resources section.)

63
Chemicals and School Performance

GOALS: ▶
- Help students understand the relationship between their chemical use and school performance
- Assess their level of school performance

DESCRIPTION: ▶

Group members use a worksheet and discussion to examine how their chemical use has affected their school performance.

DIRECTIONS: ▶

Ask group members why it is that people who use chemicals regularly are often the people who aren't doing well in school. List their reasons on the blackboard, which will likely include "Because they don't do their work," "School's boring!" and "Because they cut class."

Hand out the **Chemicals and School Performance** worksheet for them to complete. When they are finished, ask them to share their answers with the rest of the group and explain the relationship between their chemical use and school performance.

QUESTIONS: ▶
- What were your grades before you began using chemicals regularly?
- How has your chemical use affected your school performance?
- How do you feel about school?
- How did you feel about school before you started using chemicals?
- What would you like your grades to be now?
- What needs to change in order for that to happen?

MATERIALS: ▶

Chemicals and School Performance worksheet.

Chemicals and School Performance

Many people in trouble with chemicals don't see any connection between their alcohol and other drug use and their school grades and attendance. But usually there's a strong connection. Complete all three columns below by writing in your overall grade average for the year, total number of days absent from school for the year, and your honest impressions of your chemical use for that year rated on a scale of 1 to 10.

	2 years ago	Last year	This year
What were your grades? (Letter grade A - F)			
Days of school absent? (For any reason)			
Your chemical use? (Scale of 1-10 1 = none 10 = all the time)			

What is the connection between your chemical use and your school performance?

64
Chemicals and Physical Health

GOALS:

- Encourage students to assess how their chemical use has affected their physical health
- Explain some of the possible health consequences of chemical abuse

DESCRIPTION:

Students use a worksheet and discussion to assess how their chemical use has affected their physical health.

DIRECTIONS: ▶

Ask students to list some of the ways that chemical use can affect a person's physical health. If the group focuses only on the pharmacological affects, such as brain damage or physical addiction, point out to them that chemical abuse is also responsible for health problems such as accidents, stress reactions, suicide (see following page for a comprehensive list).

Pass out the worksheet on the following page. When they are finished, spend the remaining time discussing their answers.

MATERIALS: ▶

Chemicals and Physical Health worksheet.

Chemicals and Physical Health

Chemical abuse can affect our physical health in many ways. Read through the descriptions, circle those that you have experienced, and explain.

Symptom	Explanation
Losing weight	
Tired all the time	
Not enough sleep	
Malnourished	
Suicide attempt	
Self-mutilation	
Car accident	
Hurt in a fight	
Memory loss	
Shaky, jittery	
Chronic cough	
Feeling burnt out	
Hospitalization	
Sexual abuse	
Rape	
Hangover	
Frequently ill	
Sinus problems	
Needle scars	
Injured while high or drunk	
Sexually transmitted disease	

65
Assessment Questionnaire

GOALS: ▶
- Indicate students' level of chemical use
- Determine the need for future services

DESCRIPTION: ▶

Students complete and then score a self-assessment questionnaire that identifies their level of involvement with mind-altering chemicals.

DIRECTIONS: ▶

Before giving the test to group members, clarify the different categories of chemical use, misuse, abuse, and dependence by making a brief presentation (see activity #46). It's important that they understand these distinctions; otherwise, their scores on the tests won't mean much to them.

When choosing an assessment test for this activity, keep in mind that the test should be simple to both complete and score, relatively quick, yet valid and reliable. There are a number of different tests that meet these criteria (see Resources section).

After explaining the levels of chemical use and administering the test, help them to determine their scores. Once done, ask everyone, in turn, to share their scores and their position on the use—dependence continuum with the rest of the group.

Some tests have somewhat complicated scoring procedures, which might tempt you to score the tests outside of the group for the students. You'll find, though, that the activity has more impact if the students themselves do their own scoring. If more time is required, use two sessions of group, such as one to describe the use—dependence continuum and to complete the test, and one session to score their tests and discuss the results.

NOTES: ▶

Assessment of a young person's chemical dependence shouldn't be based solely on a questionnaire; instead, we need to gather information from a number of sources. This activity, and the test scores, albeit useful, are only one piece of the puzzle.

QUESTIONS: ▶
- What is your score?
- Where does your score place you on the use—dependence continuum?
- Do you think your score is accurate? Why or why not?
- If your score is inaccurate, what should your score be?

MATERIALS: ▶

Assessment questionnaire (see Resources section).

66
My Chemical Story

GOALS: ▶
- Initiate honest disclosure of chemical use
- Familiarize group leaders with students' backgrounds
- Encourage self-assessment

DESCRIPTION: ▶ Students draw a time continuum describing their past experiences with chemicals.

DIRECTIONS: ▶ Tell group members that you would like them to describe their own personal history with alcohol and other drugs on paper. Other than making sure that the events stay in chronological order, they can describe these experiences in any manner they wish, such as a linear timeline, boxed captions, or sketching people and places. Their timelines should detail all the chemicals they have used, experiences with chemicals that were especially significant, and all consequences related to their chemical use.

Give everyone a marker and a large sheet of newsprint on which to draw their stories. With senior high students, it's a good idea to give them an entire session to draw their stories, and then spend the next session discussing what they've drawn. When the group is composed of younger students without a lengthy chemical history, it's possible to complete both parts within a single session.

When sharing their chemical stories, ask two other group members to hold the newsprint up for all to see and encourage the student sharing to be honest about what he has written.

NOTES: ▶ Occasionally, a group member might see this activity as a chance to brag or sensationalize the parties he's been to or the variety of chemicals he's used. It's best to confront this right away or the group might spin off into a "Who can top this?" session. Direct this type of student to one of the consequences he's experienced—"What happened, Paul, after your dad found you drunk in his car?"—or confront the behavior directly—"Sounds like you're trying to brag about this. Is that true?"

MATERIALS: ▶ Markers and newsprint.

67
Consequences of Chemical Use

GOALS: ▶
- Help students make an association between their behaviors and consequences
- Encourage honest self-examination

DESCRIPTION: ▶ Students compile a list of a number of typical consequences for chemical abuse and then identify which consequences they have experienced.

DIRECTIONS: ▶ Using the blackboard, ask students to list consequences of chemical abuse. This list should be both comprehensive and specific, including examples such as getting kicked off the team for drinking, grounded at home because of going to a beer party, losing a girlfriend or boyfriend because of crazy behavior while drunk.

When there is a comprehensive list, ask students in turn to share with the rest of the group the consequences that they've experienced. It's important that they also explain the chemical-related behavior that precipitated the consequence—in other words, not just the fact that they got arrested, but what they were doing that caused them to get arrested.

If a student is hesitant to share her personal consequences openly, you might ask the rest of the group to list, in a good-natured manner, several consequences they know this person has experienced. It's also a good idea for you to look through group members' school records for any documented consequences so that, if they fail to mention any salient incidents, you can jog their memory.

MATERIALS: ▶ None required.

68
Assessment of Losses

GOALS: ▶
- Encourage self-assessment of personal effects of chemical use
- Help students connect their behavior with consequences

DESCRIPTION: ▶ Students list the various losses they have experienced in their personal lives due to their chemical use.

DIRECTIONS: ▶ Begin this session by asking group members to give examples of famous people—actors, sports heros, politicians—who have experienced tragedy due to their alcohol or other drug use. Usually most every group member can cite an example of a football star who was cut from the team because of drugs, or some other famous person who died in an alcohol-related car crash.

Point out to them that, although these are rather infamous examples, many young people experience losses because of their chemical use, perhaps some of them right here in this group. Hand out **My Own Losses** worksheet on the following page and, after giving them enough time to finish, spend the rest of the session discussing their answers.

MATERIALS: ▶ **My Own Losses** worksheet.

My Own Losses

Many people experience losses due to their chemical use. Some of these are tragically obvious—car crashes, divorces, being fired—but other losses are not so clear. Consider each question listed below carefully before answering. Explain your answers instead of simply answering "yes" or "no."

1. Have you ever lost a job because of your chemical use?

2. Have you ever lost a boyfriend or girlfriend because of your chemical use?

3. Have you ever been involved sexually with someone (unintentionally) while using chemicals?

4. Have you ever lost a friend because of your chemical use?

5. How has your chemical use affected your . . .

    ■ self-esteem?

    ■ happiness?

    ■ family relations?

6. List three activities you no longer do because of your chemical use.

    1)

    2)

    3)

Section F: Getting Help

Some group members will need more than a support group can provide, such as a chemical dependence treatment program or therapy; other group members will want to continue, after the group is finished, the work that they've started in the group. Activities in this section help make the bridge between your support group and the next appropriate step.

A natural place to begin this process is to expose group members to the Twelve-Step community. Alcoholics Anonymous, Narcotics Anonymous, and Alateen are available nationwide, even in rural communities. It's especially helpful for you, as a group leader, to have a practical understanding of these programs. Fortunately, this understanding is very simple to come by. Obtain a schedule of the meetings in your community and attend an *open* meeting (open meetings are open to the public, while closed meetings are for anyone with a drinking problem).

With this practical background, an understanding of the treatment centers and other resources available, and these activities, you'll be able to respond appropriately when a group member, motivated by the self-awareness you've helped create through the group experience, reaches out and says "I need some help."

69
Twelve-Step Support

GOALS: ▶

- Increase awareness of community resources
- Encourage appropriate students to begin attending Twelve-Step groups

DESCRIPTION: ▶

Students are introduced to twelve-step groups of Alcoholics Anonymous and Narcotics Anonymous through guest speakers and literature.

DIRECTIONS: ▶

Arrange for a member of a local Alcoholics Anonymous (A.A.) or Narcotics Anonymous (N.A.) group to come and speak to your support group. This can be easily accomplished by calling the contact number listed in your phone book and asking for a public speaker.

It's a good idea to discuss this topic the week previous to the speaker's presentation. Ask group members if they have had any experience with twelve-step groups before. What are their perceptions about these programs? Ask them to explain, in their own words, what purpose these groups serve. Encourage debate as this tension will stimulate questions and interest in the speaker the following week. While this discussion is taking place, appoint a member of the group to record the disagreements and questions the group is unable to answer. These questions can then be raised with the speaker.

NOTES: ▶

When requesting a speaker, ask for someone whom your group members can readily relate to—a young recovering person who abused street drugs instead of a retired person whose chemical experience was limited to alcohol. Limit this speaker's presentation so that there will be time for questions and discussion.

MATERIALS: ▶

None required.

70 Visiting a Twelve-Step Meeting

GOALS: ▶

- Increase awareness of community resources
- Encourage appropriate students to begin attending Twelve-Step groups

DESCRIPTION: ▶

Students visit an open Alcoholics Anonymous (A.A.) or Narcotics Anonymous (N.A.) meeting and discuss their experiences the following group session.

DIRECTIONS: ▶

First, you'll need to obtain a copy of the twelve-step meeting schedule for your community and identify which meetings are closed and which are open. Closed meetings are only for people who have a drinking problem—in the case of A.A.—while open meetings are for anyone to come and see what the group is all about. This includes family or friends of a member, journalists, or anyone interested in learning more about the particular twelve-step group. Usually meeting schedules designate open and closed meetings (contact your local Alcoholics Anonymous clubhouse or hotline phone number for more information).

After you know which meetings are open, request that support group members attend an open A.A. or N.A. meeting. You could organize a field trip to go to an open meeting all together or they may wish to go less formally in several smaller groupings. The following week, ask group members to discuss their impressions and experiences.

NOTES: ▶

Group members usually don't like this assignment. Often this reaction stems from fear concerning a new and unknown situation. Encouraging them to go together reduces this uneasiness. Since many group members are participating in this support group because of consequences, you could make it a requirement for completion of the group program, if necessary.

If you haven't attended a twelve-step meeting either, then you really ought to go yourself—otherwise your students will end up knowing more about it than you will. In this case, offering to take group members with you will even further reduce any anxiety.

QUESTIONS: ▶

- How were you feeling when you first entered the meeting room? And when the meeting was over?
- What did the speakers have in common?
- What was the mood in the meeting room?
- What did you hear during the meeting that was helpful for you?
- What did you hear during the meeting that you disagreed with?
- How would you describe this meeting?
- Would this group be of help to you?

MATERIALS: ▶

Twelve-step meeting schedules.

71
The Twelve Steps

GOALS: ▶
- Help students understand the Twelve Steps
- Encourage students to use the Twelve Steps to help them abstain from chemicals

DESCRIPTION: ▶

Using lecture and examples, students learn how the Twelve Steps can help people with drinking or other drug problems.

DIRECTIONS: ▶

Begin this session by giving group members copies of the Twelve Steps for Young People handout and making a brief presentation explaining these Twelve Steps (see following pages and Appendix B). After this introduction, ask group members to create a fictitious young person, whom we'll call Jack, with a chemical dependence problem. The group should set the stage by describing various aspects of Jack's chemical dependence problem, such as use patterns, affects on peer relations, school performance, family tension, and so on. It can be helpful to make notes on the blackboard. Someone may even wish to draw a picture of Jack on the blackboard.

Once Jack has been described, assign the various Steps to group members by numbering off around the circle until all Twelve Steps have been assigned (it's okay if some group members have been assigned more than one step).

Now tell the group they're going to help Jack get sober by helping him work the steps. Each group member should think about how Jack would use his or her assigned step to help himself get sober. After giving them a few minutes to think about this, ask the group member assigned the first step to describe Jack working this step. For example, "Jack didn't really want to admit that he had a drinking problem. Whenever anyone mentioned it to him, he got really angry and defensive. But one night, his girlfriend broke up with him because she had had enough of his being drunk all the time. That's when he realized he really did have a problem." Continue this process with the remaining steps.

Finish this session by asking group members to think about how the Twelve Steps would work in their lives.

NOTES: ▶

If you predict that the group will find this task difficult, you may wish to volunteer to describe Jack's work with the first step yourself in order to model desired behavior.

QUESTIONS: ▶
- Why do you think it's important to list all the wrongdoings and hurts you've caused others?
- Which step would be the most difficult for you?
- What is a higher power for you?
- Would working these steps be helpful for you? How?

MATERIALS: ▶

Twelve Steps for Young People handout.

Twelve Steps for Young People

1. I tried to be in charge of my life, but it got messed up.

2. I start trusting a higher power and other people in my life.

3. I reach out and ask for help.

4. I make a list of mistakes I've made.

5. I share my list with someone I really trust.

6. I decide I really do want things to be different for me.

7. I let my higher power and other people help me.

8. I make a list of people whom I've hurt.

9. I apologize to these people and make things right.

10. I work to correct the mistakes that I make.

11. I continue to ask my higher power for help.

12. I share my experiences with others.

For Your Information . . .

The Twelve Steps*

 The Twelve Steps are the historical and practical foundation of Alcoholics Anonymous and have since been modified for use in many other self-help groups such as Al-Anon, Narcotics Anonymous, Gamblers Anonymous, and Overeaters Anonymous. Regardless of the program, though, the Twelve Steps remain the same with the exception of what the group designates as their being powerless over in the first step. In Alcoholics Anonymous the first step reads: "We admitted that we were powerless over alcohol—that our lives had become unmanageable."

The steps are the backbone of all Twelve-Step programs, helping them get sober and then serving as a series of guidelines for living a healthy productive life. No one is finished when reaching Step Twelve but continues to practice the steps in her life.

The first three steps are about surrendering. Simply put, newcomers admit they have a problem, they see there is help available, and they ask for that help. It's the ending and beginning for a chemically dependent person: the end of the drinking or getting high, and the beginning of sobriety and a new life.

Steps four through six encourage self-assessment. People beginning to work these steps usually have left a long trail of strained relationships, school troubles, legal disputes, and personal guilt and shame. Their lives are a mess. Now it's time to begin sorting this out by making a list, coming clean by talking about the "secrets" with someone (this person might be a member of the clergy, a counselor, or a friend), and then being willing to leave all this heartache and tragedy behind and start anew.

Steps seven through nine recognize that chemically dependent people need to live in community with others. It's important that they be willing to reach out and ask for help, to take a good long look at the people they've hurt, and then to make amends.

The last three steps require action. They become an intregal part of what Twelve-Step group members refer to as their "program." Recovering people continue to correct any mistakes they make, look for direction and guidance in their sobriety, and help other struggling chemically dependent people find sobriety by reminding themselves that "We keep what we have by giving it away."

---

* For additional information on the Twelve Steps, see page 212.

72
Field Trip to a Treatment Center

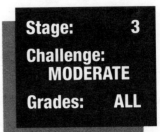
GOALS: ▶
- Challenge misconceptions about treatment centers
- Reinforce concept of chemical dependence as a disease
- Reduce anxiety of students anticipating entering a treatment program

DESCRIPTION: ▶ Support group members spend a few hours visiting a chemical dependence treatment center to become more familiar with a typical program.

DIRECTIONS: ▶ Arrange for a guided tour of a treatment center in your community. Since this isn't a typical request, make sure the information and activities will be both interesting and ageappropriate for your group members. Possible activities could include a tour of the building, a small group session, and a description of the program from start to finish.

NOTES: ▶ Most likely, you'll need parent permission slips for this activity.

MATERIALS: ▶ None required.

73
Is My Friend in Trouble?

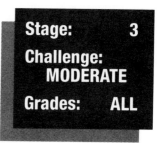

GOALS: ▶
- Help students determine if friends are in trouble with their chemical use
- Encourage self-assessment of chemical use

DESCRIPTION: ▶

Students complete an assessment instrument that helps them determine if a friend is in trouble with chemicals.

DIRECTIONS: ▶

Ask group members to think of someone close to them whose chemical use concerns them. Going around the circle, ask them to describe this person's chemical use to the group. Typically, group members will have difficulty making a judgment about the severity of the problem. They are uneasy about their friend or family member's chemical use, but they don't really know how to rate the problem.

Hand out the questionnaire on the following pages to the group members. After they have completed it, discuss the results. Ask them if the questionnaire results agree with their own opinions. Then turn the tables on them by asking what the scores would be if their friends were completing this questionnaire with the focus on them. Point out to them that they won't be of much help to their friends or family if they are in trouble with chemicals themselves.

NOTES: ▶

Activity #76, **Sharing Your Concerns**, is a natural follow-up for this activity.

MATERIALS: ▶

Is My Friend in Trouble? questionnaire.

Is My Friend In Trouble?

Answer each question by checking yes or no. Even if you can answer yes to only one part of a question that has several parts, answer the entire question with a yes.

SECTION I

Yes   No

1. Has this person ever been arrested on a MIP (Minor in Possession charge) or been at a party broken up by the police?

2. Has this person ever been suspended from school activities for using chemicals? Has this person dropped school or other activities that used to be important to him or her?

3. Do most of this person's friends use chemicals?

4. Has this person ever had a hangover or a bad trip because of chemical use?

5. Has this person ever lied to you or made excuses about chemical use?

6. Does this person experience unexplainable mood changes or emotional ups and downs?

7. Has this person ever embarrassed you or other friends because of chemical use?

SECTION II

8. Has this person ever been arrested for shoplifting, vandalism, driving while intoxicated, or possession of alcohol or other drugs?

9. Has this person ever been suspended from school for possession of chemicals or fighting?

10. Has this person stolen money from her house or stolen things that could be sold? Or stolen alcohol?

11. Has this person changed friends from those who don't use chemicals to those who do?

12. Has this person experienced a significant weight loss or gain, unexplained injuries, respiratory problems, or overdoses? Has his appearance or personal hygiene become sloppy?

13. Does it appear harder for this person to pay attenion to something or someone for a long time? Does she have less motivation than before? Has this person had memory lapses?

14. Have you heard this person say things like "I wish I were dead"?

15. Does this person strongly defend his right to drink or use other drugs?

16. Have you witnessed this person manipulating her parents to lie or cover up for her at school, at work, or with friends?

continued on next page

SECTION III

___ ___ 17. Has this person ever been arrested for robbery, drug dealing, assault and battery, or prostitution?

___ ___ 18. Has this person been suspended from school more than once or expelled?

___ ___ 19. Has this person stayed away from home for more than a weekend, or even left home "for good"?

___ ___ 20. Has this person become violent with his friends, or started avoiding them?

___ ___ 21. Has this person experienced obvious weight loss or injuries? Has she ever overdosed, had tremens, dry heaves, or chronic coughing?

___ ___ 22. Does this person blame her parents, friends, or others for the problems she is experiencing? Does she seem to be angry all the time? Does she have trouble remembering things she said or did?

___ ___ 23. Has this person ever made suicide plans, left suicide notes, or actually attempted suicide?

___ ___ 24. Are you afraid for this person's safety because of any of the behaviors described in this questionnaire?

What your responses mean:

■ No answers to most of questions 1 - 8 indicate that this person is probably not involved in chemical use.

■ Yes answers to most of questions 1 - 8 indicate that this person is misusing chemicals.

■ Yes answers to most of questions 9 - 16 indicate that this person is probably abusing chemicals.

■ Yes answers to most of questions 17 - 24 indicate that this person is probably chemically dependent.

The information in this questionnaire was adapted from *Choices & Consequences: What to Do When a Teenager Uses Alcohol/Drugs* by Dick Schaefer (see Resources section).

74
Dear Andy

GOALS: ▶
- Find solutions for problems common to students beginning to abuse chemicals
- Learn new coping skills

DESCRIPTION: ▶ Group members read fictitious letters to an advice columnist and discuss solutions to the problems raised in these letters.

DIRECTIONS: ▶ Taking turns, students should choose and then read aloud a letter from the samples provided (see following page). After reading the letter, the group should discuss what advice it would give.

MATERIALS: ▶ **Dear Andy** letters.

Dear Andy Letters

Dear Andy:
Almost twice a week I listen to my parents fight. It's usually after dad gets drunk. (He drinks almost every night.) I try to listen to figure out who's right and who's wrong. The problem is I don't get much sleep at night and I fall asleep in class the next day. I've started getting high in my room before I go to bed so that I can sleep through their fights. I'll never be a drunk like my old man, but I'm afraid that some night they'll bust me in my room.

Matthew

Dear Andy:
Last summer, the group of friends I hang around with started drinking. Now school's started, and they still drink a lot, even though we're all on the basketball team. I still hang around them, but it's getting harder and harder to resist getting drunk right along with them. Some of them are really bad now, and I don't want to end up like them, but I still want to be friends.

Melanie

Dear Andy:
I know I've got a problem with drinking. I get drunk at least twice a week. Sometimes I drink out in my car during lunch break. My girlfriend just broke up with me because she thinks I'll end up being an alkie. I've tried to convince her I can quit any time I want, but she doesn't believe me. How can I get her back?

Lenny

Dear Andy:
My dad has a drinking problem. He doesn't live with us anymore. Since he's left, my mom is always too busy or tired to pay any attention to me. Instead she's always worrying about the bills and is sad or crabby most of the time. I feel like my dad forgot all about me and that I'm just one more problem for my mom. Now things have gotten bad at school 'cause I just don't care about homework or grades any more. My mom and me fight all the time and I feel angry, lonely, and confused.

Jorge

Dear Andy:
My older brother has a bad drug problem. Whenever our parents are gone, he's off in his room getting high or inviting friends over to party. A few days ago, they stole some liquor from my dad. He saw that it was gone and started accusing all of us kids. Now he's demanding that someone confess. My brother told me that if I say anything, he'll never speak to me again. I don't want to narc on my brother, but I don't want to be blamed either.

Tina

Dear Andy:
My best friend is really into crack—he talks about it like it's magic. Me, I like booze, but, who knows—maybe I'll like rock better. I keep hearing such bad things about it, though. Is it all just scare tactics, or should I really stay away from the stuff?

Simone

75
Enabling

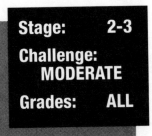

Stage: 2-3
Challenge: MODERATE
Grades: ALL

GOALS: ▶
- Help students identify enabling behaviors
- Motivate students to stop enabling friends and family

DESCRIPTION: ▶ Students discuss various enabling behaviors they have witnessed and complete an enabling inventory.

DIRECTIONS: ▶ Begin this session with a description of enabling (see **For Your Information** on page 162). It's important that everyone understands not only what enabling is, but also why it's counterproductive.

Ask the group to volunteer examples of enabling they've witnessed, such as a group member hearing his mother call in sick for his father who was really hung over, or a group member who watched a friend give a copy of her homework to another student who had been out drinking the previous night. After everyone has given an example, ask them to share a personal example of when they have enabled a friend or family member.

Now hand out the **Enabling Inventory** worksheet (see following page). When everyone has finished, discuss the scores. Spend the remaining time in the session making a list of ways that group members can avoid enabling other people, such as refusing to lie for a friend, or not making excuses for a parent's drug problem.

MATERIALS: ▶ **Enabling Inventory** worksheet.

Enabling Inventory

Answer the questions by checking the appropriate column.

No	Sometimes	Yes	
❑	❑	❑	1. I'd prefer a friend keep on using chemicals than have him meet with the school counselor.
❑	❑	❑	2. I've introduced a friend to chemicals.
❑	❑	❑	3. I've been concerned about a friend's chemical use but have been afraid to talk to her about it.
❑	❑	❑	4. I've been concerned about a friend's chemical use but haven't talked to a teacher or counselor about it.
❑	❑	❑	5. I'm afraid that if I share my concern with a friend I'll lose his friendship.
❑	❑	❑	6. I'm afraid others would think I'm a narc and that sharing my concerns about a friend would affect my reputation in school.
❑	❑	❑	7. I blame other things or people for a friend's chemical use or problem.
❑	❑	❑	8. I've protected and covered up for a friend who has a chemical problem.
❑	❑	❑	9. I avoid being around chemical users I'm worried about.
❑	❑	❑	10. I'm not able to break up with my boyfriend or girlfriend even though his or her chemical use causes me problems.

The information in this inventory was adapted from *From Peer Pressure to Peer Support* by Shelley MacKay Freeman (see Resources section).

For Your Information . . .

Enabling

When we do something that's harmful to ourselves or others, we often experience some type of consequence. It's one of the ways we learn important lessons. People abusing alcohol and other drugs experience many consequences: hangovers, flunking classes, family problems, lost jobs, trouble with the police. You would think that these experiences would help them make changes in their behavior rather quickly. That's not the case, though.

The reason they don't make changes in their behaviors is because they don't experience the consequences. And the reason they don't experience consequences is because people around them—often family or friends—come to their rescue.

This is called enabling, and it's the term used to describe things people do (or don't do, for that matter) that shield a person in trouble with chemicals from experiencing the consequences they really need to feel. The classic example would be the wife calling in sick for her husband who's really just hung over. She does it for obvious reasons: doesn't want him to lose his job, get upset with her, or be in a worse mood than he already is. But, what does the husband now know? Every time he drinks too much in the evening (which is happening more frequently), he knows that his wife will come to the rescue. She wants him to quit drinking, and yet her actions allow him to drink even more: the opposite effect of what she wants!

Enabling is understandable. When we see someone we care about in trouble, we almost automatically come to their rescue. But, if we really care about someone in trouble with chemicals, we'll allow them to experience the consequences of their actions. Only after they feel this pain will they finally say "Ouch!" and make some changes in their behavior.

Here's a few more examples of enabling:
- A student letting a friend copy her homework though she knows he didn't get his done because he was out partying all weekend.
- A teacher avoiding confronting a student in his class who he thinks might be high.
- A principal calling a student in trouble with chemicals into his office and yelling at him to shape up but not getting him any help.
- Friends of a student whom they're really concerned about not saying anything because they're afraid he'll get angry.

76
Sharing Your Concerns

GOALS: ▶
- Encourage students to confront their friends who are in trouble with chemicals
- Teach students how to express themselves in a manner that people can hear

DESCRIPTION: ▶

Students learn basic confrontation techniques and role-play situations similar to personal concerns.

DIRECTIONS: ▶

Ask group members to think of someone they are close to who is in trouble with chemicals, and on a piece of paper write three behaviors related to this person that concern them. Go around the circle, asking group members if they've ever told this person their concerns. Most will say no. Ask them why they haven't shared their concerns and discuss their answers, which typically include "I'm afraid he'd get angry," "It's not really any of my business," "She'd deny it all."

Use this opportunity to teach group members how to communicate their concerns in a manner that will be heard by their friend or family member. Typically, we all share our concerns with statements like this: "You drink too much," or "If you don't quit getting high, you're going to flunk your classes." Unfortunately, this automatically puts the person on the defensive and leads to arguing and minimizing. Demonstrate this by asking for a volunteer to sit in the center of the circle and pretend to be someone who's in trouble with alcohol and other drugs. Then ask everyone to share his or her concerns with this person in the center, pretending this person is the one whom they're concerned about. Expect lots of arguing, defensiveness, and frustration. In short, this method doesn't work very well.

There's a better way. The communication framework to use is this: "I feel (name a feeling) when you (describe a behavior)." For example: "I feel sad when I see you staying stoned all the time," "I feel angry when we were supposed to be going out on a date and instead all you do is get drunk with your friends," "I feel scared when you get drunk and start yelling at mom." When you communicate something by owning your own feelings, it has a powerful effect. How can someone argue with that? They can't tell you that you don't feel that way!

Now ask group members to do the same role-play, only this time everyone should phrase their concerns with "I" statements. Afterwards, discuss how much more effective this approach is. Finish this session by asking the group if they are going to approach their friend or family member with their concerns. Follow up on this during the next session of group by asking them how it went.

continued on next page

QUESTIONS: ▶

- Who is the person you are concerned about?
- Have you ever tried to share your concerns? What happened?
- Will you be able to share your concerns now using "I" statements?
- How do you think these concerns will be heard?
- Is there anyone else who's also concerned about this person?
- Could you share these concerns together?

NOTES: ▶

If there's someone in the group who isn't concerned about anyone (or at least makes that statement), this person would be a good choice for the center role. If everyone has concerns, either take this center role on yourself, or have students take turns so that all have a chance to practice "I" statements.

MATERIALS: ▶

Paper.

Section G: Goals and Decisions

Many group members will be able to set and reach personal goals; other group members will not. Is there a contradiction here? Not really. Those young people who aren't yet deeply involved with chemicals can consider what they want for themselves, plan realistic goals, and work towards them. That's what the activities in this session are all about.

On the other hand, these activities will sail right over the heads of those group members who are, because of their own chemical dependence, unable to keep goals and commitments. These unmet commitments, while personally frustrating, can be used in the confrontation process to help chemically dependent teenagers see that they are, in fact, out of control of their chemical use and, ultimately, their lives. Up until this point, they're apt to say "It's not a problem for me, 'cause I've got things under control." A group member's failure to keep goals and decisions she laid out for herself, with the best of intentions, proves otherwise.

These activities aren't designed to set group members up for failure; on the contrary, they're designed to help group members succeed by teaching them how to set goals and also how to recognize and remove their personal stumbling blocks. Talking about their feelings, being assertive with peers, abstaining from alcohol and other drugs—the skills group members need to meet these goals are outlined in this section.

77
Making Choices

GOALS: ▶
- Learn decision-making technique
- Practice decision-making process

DESCRIPTION: ▶ Students learn about, and then practice, healthy decision-making skills using real-life problems.

DIRECTIONS: ▶ Introduce this activity by encouraging group members to describe problems they've had in the past in which they had to decide on a course of action for a specific dilemma. Examples might include deciding whether to drink alcohol at a party, how to handle an overbearing friend, or what to do about the drinking problem of a family member.

Before group members complete the worksheet (see following page) explain the different steps to the decision-making process, using an example that you or the group selects and the worksheet as a guide. Once they understand the different steps, ask them to complete step one on the worksheet.

After everyone has identified a problem they don't know how to handle, go around the group circle and ask everyone to share the problem he or she chose in step one. When a group member shares her problem, each member of group should volunteer a possible solution. She should write all these suggestions in step two. Steps three and four of the worksheet can then be completed individually. When everyone has finished step four, ask the group to share their worksheets. Challenge them to follow through on their chosen course of action sometime before the next group session so that, during the following session, the outcomes can be discussed and the final step of the worksheet can be completed.

MATERIALS: ▶ **Making Choices** worksheet.

Making Choices

STEP ONE: What is the problem?

STEP TWO: What are your possible choices? (Ask the group.)

1 -

2 -

3 -

4 -

5 -

STEP THREE: Think about your choices.

POSITIVE ASPECTS   **NEGATIVE ASPECTS**

1 -

2 -

3 -

4 -

5 -

STEP FOUR: Decide which choice is the best for you.

STEP FIVE: Follow though on this choice.

STEP SIX: Afterwards, reflect on the choice you made.

- Looking back, was this really the best choice?
- Will you do anything different next time you're in this situation?

78
Setting Goals

GOALS: ▶
- Encourage goal setting
- Teach problem-solving skills

DESCRIPTION: ▶
Group members complete a worksheet that helps them clarify and work towards a personal goal.

DIRECTIONS: ▶
Begin this session by asking group members to choose a personal problem they are experiencing, such as fighting with parents or quitting getting high, that they would like to change. After everyone has shared their problem with the rest of the group, hand out the **Setting Goals** worksheet (see following page) and ask them to complete it. You may wish to go over the worksheet with the group beforehand to make sure they understand it.

After everyone has finished, ask them to share their work with the group. Don't hesitate to offer suggestions if a group member chooses a goal that is too difficult or outlines what he won't do rather than what he will do, for example.

Ask everyone to keep their worksheets so they can refer to them while working towards their goals. Record these personal goals for your own reference. During the next session of group students can discuss their progress towards reaching their goals.

NOTES: ▶
Instead of a one-week review, you may wish to wait several weeks, or follow up on students' progress with a brief discussion several times during the course of the group.

MATERIALS: ▶
Setting Goals worksheet.

Setting Goals

1. A problem I have:

2. What I want to change about this problem:

3. What I can do to help make this change happen:

   1 -

   2 -

   3 -

4. What I am **willing** to do to help bring about this change:

   1 -

   2 -

   3 -

5. I am willing to do this by this date:

79
Goals and Decisions

GOALS: ▶
- Reinforce personal decisions made by students
- Encourage goal setting
- Identify personal needs and issues

DESCRIPTION: ▶ Group members are asked to identify and set personal goals for themselves and share them with the rest of the group.

DIRECTIONS: ▶ Ask group members to think about the personal issues and problems they have identified as a result of participating in their support group. Pass out sheets of paper and ask them to write these personal issues in the form of a goal they can work towards. Typical examples include quitting drinking, talking more often about their feelings with friends, or learning more about how their problems with chemical dependence have affected them.

Also ask the group to think about any personal decisions they've made for themselves, such as not hanging around a particular person any longer, not smoking pot anymore, or attending Narcotics Anonymous.

After everyone has had time to write down their goals and decisions, ask group members to share their answers. Encourage the rest of the group to give feedback to a student after she has finished sharing her goals and decisions. For example, the group might remind a student about when she had told the group she really needs to go running when she gets angry at her dad when he's been drinking, instead of going out with her boyfriend and getting high. She can then add this additional goal to her list.

NOTES: ▶ This activity can be used either in the early stages of group or later on, after students have developed some awareness as to how their chemical use affects their lives. Using this activity during the initial sessions of group is beneficial in that these clarified goals will provide a sense of direction for the group. You might find, though, that students won't be able to identify personal issues or goals at this early stage. In this case, it will be better to save this activity for when the students' awareness has been raised. Or, use this activity twice and compare the goals. Group members might find their personal goals to be quite different the second time around.

MATERIALS: ▶ Paper.

80
How I Want to Be When I Grow Up

GOALS: ▶
- Encourage students to set personal goals
- Draw attention to importance of emotional health

DESCRIPTION: ▶

Students describe what kind of people they want to be ten years from now (happy, confident, mature, sensitive) and discuss what steps need to be taken to ensure this will happen.

DIRECTIONS: ▶

Point out to the group that when we discuss the future, we often think in terms of where we want to live or what we want to be doing—"What do you want to be when you grow up?" The focus of this activity is, instead, not where or what but how do you want to be when you grow up. Do you want to be someone that others turn to for help? Someone that little children like? Do you want to be quiet and thoughtful or the life of the party? Years from now do you want to still be in trouble with alcohol and other drugs, or do you want this problem to be behind you?

Ask students to fill out the worksheet (see following page). When everyone is finished, ask them to share their answers with the group. After they have shared both the Now and Future categories, ask group members to describe what is different between the first and second category. Once a student has identified what needs changing (she wants to be more outgoing in the future, for example), ask her what needs to happen for this change to take place. If she isn't able to think of a plan, ask the group for suggestions. For example, a student might, in the future, like to be the kind of person who has his "act together," whereas now he is always in some kind of trouble. The group might suggest to him that every day he spend a few minutes talking with a good friend about how he's feeling and what he's planning on doing before he makes impulsive decisions.

NOTES: ▶

If students don't offer advice and look to you for suggestions, resist. Instead, ask another group member what she thinks this student should do to make these changes.

MATERIALS: ▶

How I Want to Be When I Grow Up worksheet.

How I Want to Be
When I Grow Up

Below, list eight examples that describe the kind of person you are now—not what you do, but who you are and what you are like. Examples could include I'm outgoing, I worry about things too much, I'm a burnout, I'm a good listener.

1)_____

2)_____

3)_____

4)_____

5)_____

6)_____

7)_____

8)_____

Okay, now think about the kind of person you'd like to be ten years from now. Do you want to reduce your shyness and be more outgoing? Do you want to no longer worry so much about what other people think about you? Go ahead and dream. List eight qualities you would like to have be a part of you ten years from now:

1)_____

2)_____

3)_____

4)_____

5)_____

6)_____

7)_____

8)_____

81
From Now On

GOALS: ▶
- Encourage goal setting
- Support personal changes made by group members

DESCRIPTION: ▶
Group members review lessons they've learned about themselves during the course of group and identify new behaviors they'll continue to practice.

DIRECTIONS: ▶
Review previous sessions with the group, pointing out various lessons that have been presented. These examples might include learning that it's important to talk about your feelings, learning how to say no, learning that chemicals have caused problems. After reviewing these past lessons, ask them to reflect on the personal lessons they've learned during group. Hand out the **From Now On** worksheet (see following page). When they have finished filling it out, spend the remaining time sharing their answers.

NOTES: ▶
If there's an important personal lesson you think a group member failed to remember and record on her worksheet, bring it to her attention. For example: "What about last week, Cindy, when you realized you never have any time to spend alone. Is that something that should be included on your list of things to do from now on?"

After meeting with these students for a number of sessions, you probably will have specific concerns about some members of the support group. For example, you might notice that Danny often talks about how he gets upset when his parents are arguing, or that Betsy continues to be defensive about her drinking. If these students do not address these issues on their worksheets, you should bring it to their attention.

MATERIALS: ▶
From Now On worksheet.

From Now On

On this worksheet list the things that you will do differently based on what you have learned in your support group.

From now on, I'm going to	Instead of

From now on, I'm going to	Instead of

From now on, I'm going to	Instead of

From now on, I'm going to	Instead of

From now on, I'm going to	Instead of

82
Stumbling Blocks

GOALS: ▶
- Help students identify things that interfere with making positive changes
- Discuss methods for coping with this interference

DESCRIPTION: ▶
Students identify and discuss those things in their lives that prevent them from making positive changes.

DIRECTIONS: ▶
Begin this session by asking the group to define what is meant by "taking care of yourself." If need be, steer them in the direction of defining this concept as all those things you do that are healthy, positive, and affirming. This includes everything from attending classes to following curfew, talking about their feelings to confronting someone when they are upset with their behavior, quitting getting high to dealing with stress constructively. Ask the group if they're always successful in taking care of themselves. Of course, the answer to this question will be no. Tell them that you have a worksheet for them to complete that will help them understand what interferes with their ability to be good to themselves (see following page). After everyone has completed the worksheet, spend the remaining time discussing their answers.

QUESTIONS: ▶
- How many of you have similar stumbling blocks?
- What are these common stumbling blocks?
- Have you always had stumbling blocks in your life?
- Why or why not?
- Have you tried to get rid of these stumbling blocks before?
- Were you successful?

MATERIALS: ▶
Stumbling Blocks worksheet.

Stumbling Blocks

For each block below fill in something that interferes with your being able to take care of yourself. These stumbling blocks might include a certain friend, cocaine, not getting enough sleep, cigarettes, a girlfriend, or television, for example.

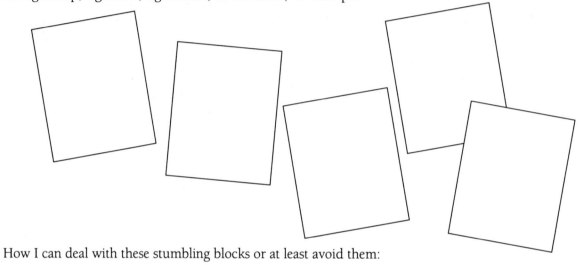

How I can deal with these stumbling blocks or at least avoid them:

1.

2.

3.

4.

5.

Material for this worksheet adapted from *From Peer Pressure to Peer Support* by Shelley MacKay Freeman (see Resources section).

83
What I Need to Change

GOALS: ▶
- Identify conditions that must be changed before students can successfully quit using chemicals
- Encourage constructive peer influence

DESCRIPTION: ▶

The support group as a whole outlines for each student the conditions that should be changed in order for that particular student to be able to quit using chemicals.

DIRECTIONS: ▶

Begin this session by asking group members to list on the blackboard the things that would get in the way for someone who was trying to quit drinking and getting high, such as hanging around friends who got drunk all the time, going to a party where lots of drugs would be available, skipping school, avoiding talking about what was going on inside, being stressed out all the time.

Once they have made an extensive list, ask for a group member to volunteer to be "it." Assuming the group is familiar with this person's background, ask the rest of the group to identify what this person must change in order to quit using chemicals. Often the group will be hesitant to speak out. In this case start around the circle and request that each person name one thing that should be changed. Ask one group member to be the recorder. He should write down all these suggestions on a piece of paper to give to the group member who is being given feedback. If the person who is "it" becomes defensive, trying to debate the suggestions offered, tell her she'll be given a chance to speak after everyone has finished making suggestions; until that time she should remain quiet. Be sure to share your suggestions also.

When the group has finished offering suggestions to this person, ask her to choose who the group will focus on next.

NOTES: ▶

This activity requires that group members be familiar with each other's background and personal lives in order to be successful.

MATERIALS: ▶

Paper.

84
What Would Change If You Quit?

GOALS: ▶
- Identify positive results of quitting using chemicals
- Encourage students to quit using chemicals

DESCRIPTION: ▶ Students examine how their lives would change if they were to quit using alcohol and other drugs.

DIRECTIONS: ▶ Ask group members to list on the blackboard the positive things that can happen when a person quits using chemicals. Typical examples include: gets better grades, less arguments at home, no chance of getting busted, have more money.

Once a comprehensive list has been made, ask students to write down on a piece of paper at least five things that would change for them personally if they were to quit using chemicals. Once everyone has finished, ask them to share their answers with the group and to explain why and how the change would take place.

NOTES: ▶ If someone is unable or unwilling to outline any positive changes that would take place if he was to quit, ask the rest of the group to suggest things that they think would change for him.

MATERIALS: ▶ Paper.

85
The Last Word

GOALS: ▶
- Provide opportunity to reinforce learning
- Affirm students' positive decisions and behavior changes
- Hear students' self-assessments

DESCRIPTION: ▶

Students, after reviewing previous group activities and worksheets, make one final self-assessment and discuss future plans concerning chemical use.

DIRECTIONS: ▶

Before this session begins, gather together all the worksheets and questionnaires the students completed in previous group sessions. (This assumes you collected worksheets at the end of each session—in general, a good idea.) Staple these papers in sequence so that you can hand back a packet of completed work to each group member.

Give these packets back to group members and ask them to look the information over. At this point it can be useful to ask group members to, starting with the first session, describe briefly the previous sessions of group. This will serve to help the group remember each activity and some of the lessons learned.

Once everyone has familiarized themselves with their packets, ask group members to answer these two questions:

1 - As a result of what you've learned in this group, describe the kind of problem you've had with alcohol and other drugs.

2 - What are you planning on doing about this problem?

Encourage group members to be honest. If they don't plan on doing anything about their chemical use, then they should say so. Be sure to support any positive decisions by group members.

You may also wish to ask the rest of the group to give feedback to the person who's just finished answering the two questions. This is best accomplished by going around the circle and asking everybody to give their impressions and advice after each group member answers the two questions.

MATERIALS: ▶

Worksheets from previous group sessions.

Section H: Peer Pressure

The influence of students' peer group plays a large role in group members' chemical use. During this phase in a young person's life, being liked and accepted by friends is paramount because "having friends is everything." And even when a young person in trouble with chemicals wants to break away from his cohorts, deciding he doesn't want to drink or use any longer, he usually doesn't have the slightest idea how to resist the steady peer pressure.

And why should he? He's spent the past few years as a teenager perfecting the process of being liked, accepted, "happenin'." If group members are going to make constructive changes in their behaviors, they'll need to be taught how to say no. They'll also need to practice saying no. The activities in this section provide these experiences and can be a valuable addition to your group curriculum.

86
Qualities of a Good Friend

GOALS: ▶
- Identify the qualities of a good friend
- Encourage students to build healthy friendships

DESCRIPTION: ▶

Students discuss the qualities inherent to a good friend and assess their current friendships.

DIRECTIONS: ▶

Ask the group to make a list on the blackboard of the qualities a good friend should have, such as "You can trust them," "They won't let you down," and "They make you feel good about yourself." When the group has a comprehensive list, hand out the **My Friends** worksheet (see following page) to everyone. When they've completed the worksheet, spend the remaining time discussing their answers.

QUESTIONS: ▶
- How healthy are your friendships?
- Do you spend most of your time with those friends who are good for you?
- Why do you spend time with friends who don't help you?
- How could you improve your friendships?

NOTES: ▶

Some group members might not have many friends. This in itself is important information. Ask this person "Why don't you have many friends?" "Do you wish you had more friends?" and "How does it feel to not have many friends?"

MATERIALS: ▶

My Friends worksheet.

My Friends

First list five friends below. Friend #1 should be the friend whom you spend the most time with and friend #5 should be the friend whom you spend the least amount of time with. Then write 3 positive qualities (she makes me laugh or he cares what happens to me, for example) and 3 negative qualities (she gets drunk too much or we only do what he wants to do, for example) for each friend listed.

Positive qualities	Friend's name	Negative qualities
1. 2. 3.	#1_____	1. 2. 3.
1. 2. 3.	#2_____	1. 2. 3.
1. 2. 3.	#3_____	1. 2. 3.
1. 2. 3.	#4_____	1. 2. 3.
1. 2. 3.	#5_____	1. 2. 3.

87
Considering the Alternatives

GOALS: ▶
- Help students develop critical thinking skills
- Develop a variety of ways to resist peer pressure

DESCRIPTION: ▶

Students decide on constructive responses to several scenarios involving opportunities to use alcohol and other drugs.

DIRECTIONS: ▶

Hand out the first scenario (see following pages) to all group members and ask them to read it and then respond to the questions. When everyone has finished, discuss group members' answers. Don't discourage disagreement; instead, allow them to debate different responses to the scenario. Continue with additional scenarios as time permits.

MATERIALS: ▶

Scenarios.

Scenario #1

Julie and her friends are sitting out in front of the school during lunch break when Tom drives up in his car and waves them over. They all get in and start driving around. Dave, whom Julie doesn't know very well, says "Hey, my old man's got a bunch of beer at home. Why don't we stop by my house!"

When they get to Dave's house everyone sits around in the living room and then Dave comes back with some cans of beer and passes them out to everyone, including Julie. She looks at her watch and realizes that lunch break will be over in 10 minutes.

1. What choices does Julie have?

   _____

   _____

   _____

2. What would happen with each of these choices?

   _____

   _____

   _____

3. Which choice should Julie take?

   _____

4. Why?

   _____

5. Which choice would you take in this situation?

   _____

Scenario #2

Lynn is one of the most popular kids in the school. Everybody wants to be her friend. Diane is a new kid in town and doesn't have many friends yet, so when Lynn sat down next to her in study hall, it was a surprise.

"Hey, Diane, I heard that your folks are going to be out of town for a week."

"Yeah, they're going to go see my older brother in Los Angeles."

"Huh. Well, me and a bunch of friends have been looking for a place to have a small party on Friday and I was wondering if you wanted to have a party at your house. You wouldn't have to supply the booze or anything like that . . . it's all taken care of."

1. What choices does Diane have?

_____

_____

_____

2. What would happen with each of these choices?

_____

_____

_____

3. Which choice should Diane take?

_____

4. Why?

_____

5. Which choice would you take in this situation?

_____

Scenario #3

Rita and Manuel have been going out for almost 6 months now. Sometimes they go to parties together; other times they just hang out and watch TV at his place. She really likes Manuel because he is nice to her and she trusts him. Tonight they are at a party and Manuel's been drinking a lot of wine coolers. There's this new guy who keeps hanging around Manuel and they are whispering and joking about something. Soon Manuel comes over to Rita.

"Hey, babe, look what I got here." He holds up a baggie with three rocks of crack. "Let's you and me go smoke."

"Uh-uh, Manuel. I don't want to do any of that stuff."

Manuel looks both hurt and angry. "I just paid good money for this stuff and I'm going to go smoke—with or without you. So what's the story—you coming?"

1. What choices does Rita have?

   _____

   _____

   _____

2. What would happen with each of these choices?

   _____

   _____

   _____

3. Which choice should Rita take?

   _____

4. Why?

   _____

5. Which choice would you take in this situation?

   _____

88
A Peer Pressure Continuum

GOALS: ▶

- Identify different types of peer pressure
- Develop constructive solutions for resisting difficult peer pressure situations

DESCRIPTION: ▶

Students construct a continuum of personal peer pressure experiences and identify constructive solutions for each situation.

DIRECTIONS: ▶

Pass out the **Peer Pressure** worksheet (see following page) and ask group members to complete the first part (listing four situations where peer pressure is a factor).

After everyone has finished, go around the circle and ask group members to read aloud their personal situations. Typical examples will include being asked if you want to skip class and go get high, or being called weird because you won't snort coke with everyone else. After hearing other examples, some group members might wish to change some of their own. Then they should complete the second part of the worksheet by listing constructive ways of dealing with this peer pressure. Tell group members that it's okay if they can't think of a way to deal with a specific instance of peer pressure. In that case, they should leave that number blank and go on to the next situation.

When everyone is finished with the second part, ask them to describe how they could handle each of the four instances of peer pressure. Typical examples could include telling the person she can't because she's on the volleyball team, or just walking away. If someone was unable to think of a solution for a particular instance, ask the rest of the group for suggestions.

QUESTIONS: ▶

- Will you be able to follow through with your solutions for dealing with peer pressure when you're asked to drink or get high?
- Are some methods of handling peer pressure better than others? Do you think that peer pressure is different now than it was for your parents? Why or why not?

MATERIALS: ▶

Peer Pressure worksheet.

Peer Pressure

On the top half of the line, write four examples of situations when you've felt pressured by your peers to use alcohol or other drugs. Example #1 should be an example that was very easy to deal with; example #4 should be the most difficult instance of peer pressure you've experienced.

easy to handle

very hard to handle

Now on the bottom half of this line, write how you could resist the peer pressure in each example up above the line.

89
Learning How to Say "No"

GOALS: ▶
- Identify ways to resist peer pressure to use alcohol and other drugs
- Practice using these new skills

DESCRIPTION: ▶

Students identify, through group discussion and with help from the group leader, techniques for resisting peer pressure to use alcohol or other drugs. These new skills are practiced through role-playing.

DIRECTIONS: ▶

After introducing the topic, ask students to list different methods for resisting peer pressure to use alcohol or other drugs. Ask a group member to record these examples on the blackboard. The examples can be both strategies the students have used before or ideas they think would work. Typical examples include saying "No thanks. I don't feel like it," walking away from the person offering the beer or joint, or saying "Naw. I've got to go home in an hour." If the group is having difficulty suggesting examples, ask them to think of a particular situation first and then think of the response. Ask them how they would handle someone offering them a joint out in the school parking lot or at a party, for example.

Once they've listed a number of ways to resist peer pressure on the board, the group should choose one to role-play. Ask for volunteers for the various parts: one student to say no, a student to offer the beer or joint, and several others to play supporting roles, such as other people at the party.

Once the roles are assigned, give the group members a few minutes to create a short role-play. You might want to tell them to go over into the corner of the room, away from the rest of the group, to work out the details. When they are ready, they should act out the scenario for the rest of the group.

When they have finished the role-play, discuss the scenario with the group. Has anyone in group been in this type of situation before? Was it difficult or easy to handle? What are some other responses that could be used in this situation?

Depending on the remaining time, act out new situations from the list on the blackboard with different group members.

NOTES: ▶

If your support group members are having a tough time getting into the character of their roles, you could help out by getting out there and playing a role, too. It can also be helpful to select group members who are natural clowns for the initial role-play. You might also provide props to make the scene realistic: an empty beer can, taped party music, a steering wheel.

MATERIALS: ▶

Theatrical props, if desired.

Section I:
Stress Activities

Stress isn't a problem reserved for adults. Young people experience it, too. And their coping styles and ability or inability to deal with stress parallels our own. Tests, beginning junior or senior high school, preparing for college, relationship difficulties, family problems, hormonal changes, acute peer pressure, extremely negative self-perceptions, and just figuring out how to grow up are all potential sources of stress. Unfortunately, many adolescents have turned to alcohol and other drugs to relieve, at least for a brief time, their stress.

In order to quit using chemicals to medicate their stress, we need to show them a different way to manage stress. The activities in this section provide a variety of approaches. Two popular techniques, deep muscle relaxation and positive imagery, have been proven successful for lots of people and in many situations.

90
My Coping Style

GOALS: ▶
- Identify helpful coping strategies
- Identify student stressors that require new responses

DESCRIPTION: ▶
Students complete a worksheet that provides a focus for discussing how they deal with everyday pressures.

DIRECTIONS: ▶
Pass out **My Coping Style** worksheet and ask students to complete it. When they are finished, ask a group member to read her coping response to the first item of the list. Ask the rest of the group if anyone else reacts similarly. Ask these students to stand together outside of the group circle. Then ask one of the students still seated to share his response to the first pressure on the list. Again form a grouping of students who had a similar response. Continue this process until everyone is either in a small grouping or standing alone.

While everyone is still standing, discuss the merits of their coping responses. Encourage debate between the subgroups. When finished, ask group members to return to their seats and begin this process again, using the second question on the worksheet.

QUESTIONS: ▶
(Direct these questions to the subgroups.)
- What is helpful about your coping response? What are the drawbacks?
- Does your response get rid of the stressful event?
- Which of the subgroups' coping responses is the most helpful?
- Which coping responses should you avoid using?

MATERIALS: ▶
My Coping Style worksheet.

My Coping Style

Consider your usual reactions when you answer the following questions.

When I'm:	
1. Hearing my parent's fight,	I cope by . . .
2. Being picked on,	I cope by . . .
3. Feeling disappointed,	I cope by . . .
4. Feeling embarrassed,	I cope by . . .
5. Feeling angry,	I cope by . . .
6. Late for school,	I cope by . . .
7. Feeling lonely,	I cope by . . .
8. Being accused of something,	I cope by . . .
9. Fighting with my parents,	I cope by . . .
10. Feeling nervous and anxious,	I cope by . . .

91
Coping with Stress Goals

GOALS: ▶
- Evaluate personal stress level
- Learn variety of stress-reducing techniques

DESCRIPTION: ▶

Group members discuss a number of strategies for reducing stress in their lives.

DIRECTIONS: ▶

Begin a discussion about stress—where it comes from and what happens to us when we're feeling it—by asking students to identify common stress-producing events, such as taking a test, going to a new school, or hassles at home. Then ask them to describe what happens when stress builds up in their bodies. Examples can include sleeplessness, stomachaches, irritability.

Ask the group to make a list of different things they do when they're feeling stressed and record them on the blackboard. At this point, don't judge the effectiveness of offered strategies. Typical examples include drinking or getting high, staring at the wall, fighting, talking about the stress, screaming into a pillow. When they're finished offering examples, ask the group to decide which of the strategies are counterproductive—that is, either don't reduce the stress or may even increase it. For example, drinking or getting high only postpones having to deal with the problem, screaming at others when tense produces guilt and additional stress, staring at the wall and brooding is a passive response that does little to alleviate the problem. Erase the examples that the group agrees are counterproductive.

For the remaining activities, ask the person who mentioned the example to give an example of how he uses it in his life—under what circumstances and what the outcome is. When all the remaining examples have been discussed, ask group members to choose one strategy to use the next time they are feeling stressed. Discuss the strategies they chose and in which situations they will use it.

NOTES: ▶

If the group isn't able to offer many different strategies for dealing with stress, be prepared to suggest some yourself. Here's a partial list: Running, talking with a friend, screaming into a pillow, writing in a journal, limiting responsibilities, spending all day in a park, snoozing in the sun, playing sports, meditating, practicing relaxation, yoga, deep breathing, day dreaming, reading a joke book, hanging out with friends.

MATERIALS: ▶

None required.

92
Positive Imagery

GOALS: ▶
- Increase positive thinking patterns
- Reduce stressful feelings

DESCRIPTION: ▶
Group members are taught how to practice imagining positive thoughts about themselves and personal situations.

DIRECTIONS: ▶
Introduce the concept of critical and negative self-talk by listing some examples of how people are so quick to put themselves down and judge themselves harshly. It would be especially helpful for you to give any personal examples of your own negative self-talk. Common examples include "I'll never get it right," "I'm not as attractive as she is," or "I'll probably mess up this speech I have to give in front of the class." Ask group members to share examples of their own negative thinking.

Tell the group that since these negative thoughts can affect both their feelings and behavior, you are going to teach them a method for thinking positive thoughts and imagining positive outcomes for situations in which they are involved.

First, ask group members to think of situations or common thought patterns in which they usually envision a negative outcome or are self-critical, such as worrying whether their friends like them, thinking that their parents are never going to quit drinking, or thinking that they are ugly. Then read the **Positive Imagery Script** on the following page.

After the positive imagery exercise, when everyone is back together in a circle, ask them to discuss their imaginary journeys. Tell the group they can use positive imagery whenever they are worrying about something, or are giving themselves negative messages. All it takes is a minute or two to imagine a different, positive outcome.

QUESTIONS: ▶
- What was the negative situation you imagined?
- What was the positive outcome for your situation?
- How did that outcome feel?
- Was it difficult to imagine a positive ending?

MATERIALS: ▶
Positive Imagery Script.

Positive Imagery Script

First, they all need to find a spot, preferably on the floor, where they can be comfortable. Once everyone is settled, read the following script to them:

"I want you to close your eyes and move your body around a bit to make sure that you are settled and comfortable. Now breathe in deeply and slowly a few times. Each time you exhale, feel your body getting a little heavier and heavier. Imagine the tension in your body being exhaled right along with each breath. (Give them 20 seconds or so to relax.)

"Now that you are relaxed, I want you to imagine the situation that you are worried about. Place yourself back in this situation. Imagine your surroundings, any other people who are present, the colors, the sounds. Now instead of things going wrong, imagine a great finish to this situation—the best possible outcome. You're happy, everything works out, there's nothing left to worry about. Stay with these good feelings for a minute. (Give them a minute or so to do this task.)

"Now, I want you to come back to this group room. Listen to the sounds you hear in this room, go ahead and stretch a little if you want to. When you feel ready, open your eyes and join the group circle."

93
Where's the Stress in My Body?

GOALS: ▶
- Identify stressors
- Create awareness of personal reaction to stress
- Learn how to deal with stress

DESCRIPTION: ▶ Students draw outlines of their bodies and then locate and write descriptions of how stress feels to them.

DIRECTIONS: ▶ Begin a discussion about stress, focusing on how our physical bodies can react to stress. Students may describe stress manifested in their bodies as headaches, knotted stomachs, or pain in their lower back, for example.

Pass out large sheets of newsprint and ask group members to trace each other's body outline on the paper. When finished, ask them to write the different stressors they experience on the outside of their body outline, and then to describe the different ways in which their bodies respond to stress with arrows, pictures, and words. For example, a student might identify tests, her father, dating, and starting a new class as stressors. On the paper she might draw an arrow to her forehead and describe the headaches she gets whenever she is feeling uptight about the money troubles at home, and then draw arrows to her fists and describe how she always clenches her fists when she is nervous.

After everyone has finished, use the remaining time to discuss the drawings, asking group members to think of positive methods they use to deal with their stress.

QUESTIONS: ▶
- How does stress feel to you?
- How can you tell when you're stressed?
- What situations are stressful for you?
- What do you do when you're stressed? Does this help?
- What else can you do to relieve your stress?
- What are common stress-related physical complaints and illnesses? Do you experience any of these?

MATERIALS: ▶ Large sheets of newsprint, markers.

94
Stress Reduction Through Relaxation

GOALS: ▶
- Evaluate personal stress level
- Learn stress-reducing techniques

DESCRIPTION: ▶

Group members are taught a muscle relaxation exercise as a way to reduce stress in their lives.

DIRECTIONS: ▶

Introduce the concept of stress to the group by asking them for examples of stress-producing situations such as a test, going to a new school or parents getting divorced. Ask them to describe how stress feels and where it locates itself in their bodies, such as a tight stomach or a headache, for example. Then ask them to describe what happens when stress builds up in their bodies such as sleeplessness, ulcers, irritability.

Point out to the group that oftentimes people use chemicals to relieve their stress. Adults have a couple of cocktails to calm their "nerves" or young people get high so they can "mellow out." But this is only a temporary relief. Tell the group that you are going to teach them how they can relax their bodies without using chemicals by relaxing their muscles. Point out to them that they can't be relaxed and stressed at the same time, so if they can learn to relax when feeling stressed, the tension will disappear.

Ask everyone to find a comfortable spot on the floor to lie down. They should be flat on their backs, arms at their sides. Remind them that the purpose of this activity isn't to fall asleep but to experience deep relaxation. Now read in a slow, steady voice the **Muscle Relaxation Script** on the following page. After the relaxation activity is finished, bring the group back together and ask them to discuss how this activity felt.

Point out to the group that they can bring about this feeling of deep relaxation more and more quickly if they practice. Once they're proficient with this technique, they can relax their bodies and get rid of stress in many stressful situations, such as before a test, a speech in front of the class, or when things are tense at home.

Ask the group for suggestions as to when they could practice this activity, such as at night before falling asleep, or for ten minutes after school several times each week.

NOTES: ▶

Hopefully your group room is carpeted; if not, bring pillows so the hard floor will be bearable. Chairs are the least-desirable alternative.

MATERIALS: ▶

Muscle Relaxation Script.

Muscle Relaxation Script

"I am going to give you some instructions that will help you relax your muscles, starting with your arm muscles and ending with the muscles in your legs. For each set of muscles, I'm going to ask you to tighten them for a few seconds and then let them relax. As this happens, your body will begin to feel more and more relaxed and your breathing will slow. Remember, though, the goal is to relax your body, not fall asleep. Let your mind wander and drift among peaceful thoughts and enjoy the activity. Let's begin.

"Make sure you're in a comfortable position. If you aren't, move around a bit. **(Wait for them to get adjusted.)** Now close your eyes and concentrate on your breathing. Take in a deep breath until you feel your lungs expand. And now exhale. Now again breathe in deep . . . and then exhale. Feel your heart beat slowing and your body calming. Breathe in deep, deeper . . . and exhale. **(Pause for five seconds.)**

"Now I want you to imagine an orange in your right hand. Squeeze this hand tight . . . tight . . . tighter to get every last drop of juice . . . and now drop the orange out of your hand and let your hand fall limp at your side. Notice the difference between the tension and the relaxation. This is how many of the muscles feel in our body when we're stressed and uptight . . . and often without us even realizing it. Now pick up another orange with your right hand and squeeze it, tight . . . tight . . . tighter . . . and then drop the orange and notice your hand feels even more relaxed.

"Now let's work on your left hand. **(Repeat with the same instruction as for the right hand.)**

"Now you're going to stretch your arm and shoulder muscles by raising your arms up high behind your head. Join your hands together up behind your head and, while keeping them close to the floor, stretch them up behind your head like a cat stretching after an afternoon nap. Feel the tension in you arms and shoulders. Now hold that tight . . . tight . . . tighter . . . and then relax and bring your arms to your sides. Feel how relaxed and limp your arms are now. **(Pause a few seconds and repeat.)**

"Now let's focus on your neck muscles. Just like a turtle pulling its head into its shell, bring your head down into your shoulders, tight . . . tight . . . tighter . . . and now relax. (Pause a few seconds and repeat.)

"Now let's relax some of the muscles on your face. I want you to clench your jaw muscles by gritting your teeth together. Feel how tight your jaw muscles get when you do this? Clench them tight now . . . tight . . . tighter . . . and now relax and feel your jaw sag. **(Pause a few seconds and then repeat.)**

"Oftentimes, our stomachs can get knotted up when we are feeling stress, so let's relax the muscles in the middle of our body. Imagine yourself about to be punched in the stomach and so you make your stomach muscles very tight. Hold it tight . . . tight . . . tighter . . . and now relax. Take a few slow deep breaths now, breathing in deep and then exhale . . . again breath in . . . and exhale. Now tighten your stomach again . . . tight . . . tight . . . tighter . . . and now relax. Again concentrate on your breathing. You're feeling very relaxed now. You're body is heavy; you're muscles loose

continued on next page

and very relaxed. You're breathing very slow and steady.

"Now let's concentrate on your leg muscles. Starting with your right leg, I want you to tighten these muscles by stretching your leg out as far as it will go. Imagine that you are making yourself another foot taller because your leg is stretching out so far. Hold these muscles tight . . . tight . . . tighter . . . and now let them relax. **(Pause a few seconds and repeat.)**

"Now let's do the same thing with your left leg. Tighten your left thigh muscle tight . . . tight . . . tighter . . . and then relax. **(Pause a few seconds and repeat.)**

"Your feet also have lots of muscles that need relaxing. Clench the muscles of your right foot by imagining yourself trying to pick up a softball with your toes. Clench your right foot muscles tight . . . tight . . . tighter . . . and now let them relax. **(Pause a few seconds and repeat.)**

"And now let's finish with your left foot. Try to pick up another softball with your toes. Clench these muscles tight . . . tight . . . tighter . . . and then let them relax. **(Pause a few seconds and repeat.)**

"Now let's return to your breathing. Feel how slow and steady your chest rises and falls. You body feels so heavy and your muscles so loose. Pure relaxation! Now I'll be quiet and give you a few minutes to enjoy this feeling. Let your mind drift and your breathing slow and I will speak again in a few minutes (Give the group a few minutes to enjoy their relaxation and then ask them to open their eyes and slowly sit up.) **"**

95
Good Times Without Chemicals

GOALS: ▶
- Expose students to a variety of alternative highs
- Encourage students to begin to have fun without chemicals

DESCRIPTION: ▶ Group members discuss ways to have fun without using chemicals and make a commitment to try one new activity that was discussed.

DIRECTIONS: ▶ Point out to the group that many young people who have been heavily involved with alcohol and other drugs don't know any other way of having a good time than to get high or drunk. Challenge the group to make a list on the blackboard of all the ways they can think of to have fun that don't involve chemicals. If necessary, also include guidelines that prohibit recreation that is harmful to self, other people, or property. When a group member gives an example, ask her to describe a time that she has participated in that form of recreation. For example, a group member might offer skiing as an example of something to do that doesn't involve chemicals; then she should describe a time that she went skiing and the fun she had. Besides the dramatic and exciting examples that the group will typically name, ask them to also think of examples that are easy to do, have no or little cost, and are readily available, such as going bike riding with a friend, seeing a good movie, playing the guitar, kicking the hackie sack.

Once there's a comprehensive list on the board (don't hesitate to help out if they miss any obvious examples), ask group members to pick an example from the list they haven't experienced before that they would be willing and able to try during the next several weeks. Make sure the group understands you're asking them to make a commitment to do this activity, and that they should pick an activity that will be possible for them to try. Choose one of the following group sessions to discuss the results of their activities, so group members know they have a deadline for completing the activity. During this follow-up session, ask group members to describe their activities and how they felt about it.

QUESTIONS: ▶
- Was this activity enjoyable? What did you like about it?
- Is this something that you will do again? Why or why not?
- What's different about recreation without chemicals as compared to recreation with chemicals?
- What are the negative aspects of using chemicals while recreating?
- Is it difficult to have a good time without drinking or getting high?

MATERIALS: ▶ None required.

Section J:
Group Challenge Activities

Passivity, despair, powerlessness, frustration . . . these words have a familiar ring to them when describing the disease of chemical dependence and, unfortunately, when describing young people in trouble with chemicals. Unknowingly, caregivers can end up with a group interaction style that reinforces this passivity. After all, even our designated role as caregiver can easily be misconstrued as denoting a relationship wherein we give and the students receive.

Of course we're there to give care to group members. But not exclusively. We must also empower. One way to empower young people is to get them involved in doing something, making something, changing something. Instead of struggling alone, support groups are about helping students reach out and connect with each other. When they function as a group, they can offer each other insight, hope, and motivation to change. The activities in this last section give a collection of mixed-up adolescents something to do, and, more importantly, something they must do as a group.
And when they realize they can do something positive as a group, these young people begin to realize they can do something for themselves also, that they are the ones who have power over their lives. Step by step, they begin to get their lives back on a constructive, healthy path.

96
Ask the Question

GOALS: ▶
- Encourage discussion of important and relevant issues
- Increase the trust level of the group

DESCRIPTION: ▶

Group members take turns asking each other questions relevant to the group experience.

DIRECTIONS: ▶

Explain to the group that the purpose of this activity is to find out more about each other and to encourage discussion of issues that are important but sometimes difficult to talk about. Begin by asking the first question directed to a group member. The person who answers your question creates the next question and decides whom she would like to answer it. If the person being asked the question doesn't wish to answer, he can simply say "pass." In this case, the person asking the question can then choose a new group member.

NOTES: ▶

As long as the questions don't get too ridiculous or unproductive, resist the temptation to jump in and take charge. They need to work this out on their own.

MATERIALS: ▶

None required.

97
Group Video

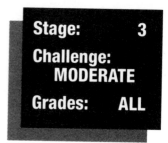

GOALS: ▶
- Increase awareness of the effects of chemical dependence
- Provide opportunities for group members to express their concerns and frustrations

DESCRIPTION: ▶

Group members make a short video dramatizing the effects of chemical dependence.

PROCEDURE: ▶

The first step is to write a script. One student should record the ideas as the rest of the group discusses possibilities for the video script. It will be helpful first to choose a focused, specific topic such as the progression of chemical dependence, how someone can get help for their drinking problem, or what school-based support groups are all about.

After the script is written, character roles should be assigned to the group members and the script rehearsed until students are comfortable with their parts. The video can then be taped by either a group member or the group leader.

NOTES: ▶

This activity will probably require three sessions: one for writing the script, another for taping the video, and the third for viewing and discussion. Encourage students to take most of the responsibility for this project. Group members shouldn't play themselves in the video because it's much easier to act out roles other than their own. And keep in mind that the main purpose of this activity is to provide a constructive outlet for students to express their concerns, not to make a slick, professional video.

MATERIALS: ▶

Video equipment such as a camera, tripod, tapes, VCR, and monitor.

98
The Student Take-over

GOALS: ▶
- Encourage students to take responsibility for their group
- Encourage students to think about their needs

DESCRIPTION: ▶
Group members are given the opportunity to plan and then facilitate the following week's group session.

DIRECTIONS: ▶
Inform the group that during the next week of group they are to be in charge. This means deciding what the focus should be, what activity they should use, how they will divide responsibilities, and what materials they need. Help them plan the group session by addressing these questions in a constructive order.

First off, they need to decide what is an important group topic for them by discussing what it is that they need. Typical examples might include talking more about their feelings, learning how to handle anger, or discussing specific problems they all experience at home.

Next, they should find an activity that focuses on this topic. They might want to invent their own activity (this should be encouraged), or you could show them this book as well as suggest other ideas. The final step is to decide how to divide the responsibilities for the group activity. Of course the following week of group should be reserved for the group to follow through with their plan.

NOTES: ▶
Even though they might be disorganized, resist the temptation to rescue the group. They'll work it out . . . and after all, though it might not run smoothly, it's their plan.

MATERIALS: ▶
Activity ideas, if they request them.

99
Group Graffiti

Stage: 2-4

Challenge: LOW

Grades: ALL

GOALS:

- Encourage free expression of thoughts and feelings
- Create group unity

DESCRIPTION:

A large sheet of newsprint is taped to the group room wall for students to draw artwork and record thoughts and feelings.

DIRECTIONS: ▶

Using bulletin board paper or large sheets of newsprint, cover a large area of a wall in the group room. Tell the group that they can write and draw whatever they wish as long as it relates to their thoughts and feelings in connection with the group experience. Leave the mural on the wall until the final session of group so that each session they can continue to add to the mural.

NOTES: ▶

If you have different groups that meet in the same room, either use different walls for each or take the murals down after each session. Also keep an eye out for negative or hurtful put-downs that a group member might write on the mural.

Depending on your group room and the types of walls, you may wish to allow the group to use a small portion of the actual wall to decorate as a group project. Over the course of many groups and years, the group room wall can become a beautiful patchwork of different group members' expressions.

MATERIALS: ▶

Poster paper or newsprint and markers.

100
The Chemical Dependence Adventure Game

Stage: 2-3

Challenge: LOW

Grades: 7-9

GOALS: ▶
- Provide a creative outlet for expressing feelings
- Reinforce concepts of chemical dependence
- Promote teamwork and problem solving

DESCRIPTION: ▶ Students create a board game depicting the personal problems inherent to being chemically dependent.

DIRECTIONS: ▶ Place a large sheet of newsprint in the center of the group circle. Tell the group that you would like them to make a board game that describes the ups and downs of growing up and developing chemical dependence. This board game could be patterned after games such as *Chutes and Ladders*, *Monopoly*, or *Candyland*. However designed, the game should include pitfalls, traps, and slides that depict the misadventures these students have experienced as well as what the future could have in store if they continue to abuse alcohol and other drugs (see following page for an example). Encourage the group to be creative and split up the task equally by giving each group member an area of the newsprint to work on and deciding the rules by consensus.

Once a rough version of the board game has been designed, give them a piece of posterboard and colored markers. Now, using the newsprint as a guide, they can construct a permanent copy.

During the following session of group, the group members can play the game.

NOTES: ▶ If you have more than one support group of this type, you could swap games between the two groups. With the group's permission, you may wish to save this game as an activity for future support groups.

MATERIALS: ▶ Newsprint, posterboard, markers, dice, index cards (in case they want a draw-card pile), objects that can serve as player markers (coins, bottle caps, colored wooden squares), **Draw Card List**.

CHEMICAL DEPENDENCE ADVENTURE GAME

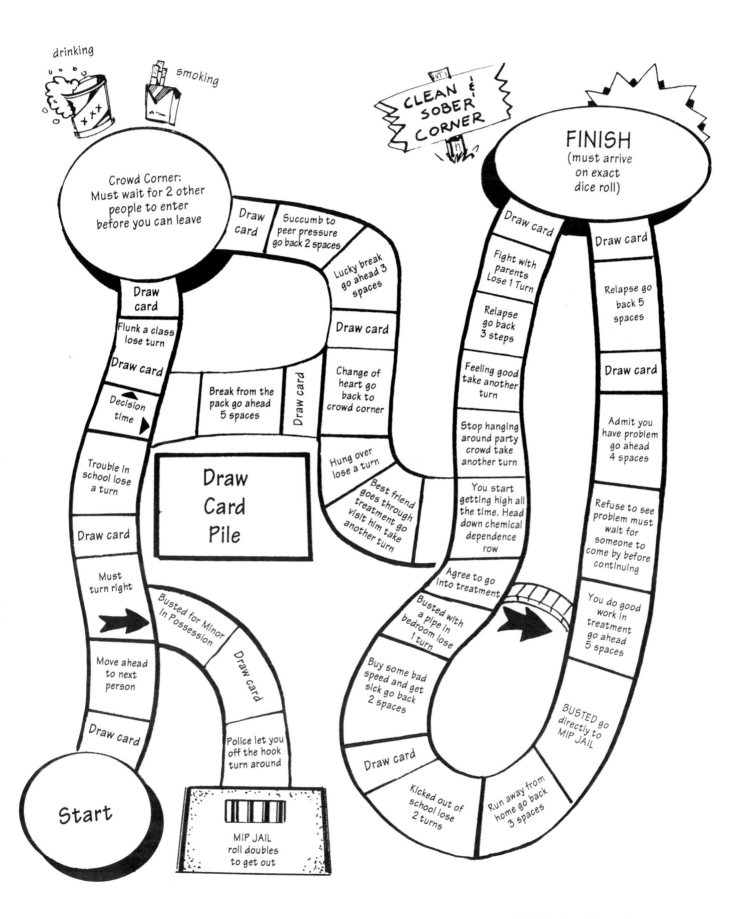

drinking

smoking

CLEAN & SOBER CORNER

Crowd Corner: Must wait for 2 other people to enter before you can leave

FINISH (must arrive on exact dice roll)

Draw card

Succumb to peer pressure go back 2 spaces

Draw card

Fight with parents Lose 1 Turn

Draw card

Relapse go back 5 spaces

Draw card

Flunk a class lose turn

Lucky break go ahead 3 spaces

Relapse go back 3 steps

Draw card

Draw card

Feeling good take another turn

Draw card

Decision time

Break from the pack go ahead 5 spaces

Draw card

Change of heart go back to crowd corner

Stop hanging around party crowd take another turn

Admit you have problem go ahead 4 spaces

Trouble in school lose a turn

Hung over lose a turn

You start getting high all the time. Head down chemical dependence row

Refuse to see problem must wait for someone to come by before continuing

Draw card

Draw Card Pile

Best friend goes through treatment go visit him take another turn

You do good work in treatment go ahead 5 spaces

Must turn right

Agree to go into treatment

Busted for Minor in Possession

Busted with a pipe in bedroom lose 1 turn

Move ahead to next person

Draw card

Buy some bad speed and get sick go back 2 spaces

BUSTED go directly to MIP JAIL

Draw card

Police let you off the hook turn around

Draw card

Kicked out of school lose 2 turns

Run away from home go back 3 spaces

Start

MIP JAIL roll doubles to get out

Draw Card List

- You decide not to get drunk with your friends, so take another turn.

- Your parents confront you about your drinking, and you storm out of the house. This defensiveness costs you a turn.

- Your drinking problem starts to interfere with your grades. Tell everybody playing the game what your grades are this semester.

- You suffer from low self-worth. Ask two people in the group to tell you something nice about yourself. Then take another turn.

- Your Dad comes home drunk and starts slapping you around. So you run away from home. Lose 2 turns.

- Your best friend starts getting high all the time. You tell him you're concerned for him. He doesn't listen, but you get to go ahead 4 spaces.

- Your parents are classic enablers. Keep this card and if you end up in MIP jail, you can get out FREE.

- You are such a good person, you pick somebody else in the game to go ahead 4 spaces.

- After getting really sick and hung over, you swear not to drink any more . . . and you mean it. Take another turn.

- You're sent for a chemical dependence assessment. Go back 9 spaces.

- You are called into the principal's office and when you get there, your parents, social worker, best friend, and favorite teacher are all there waiting for you. Intervention Time! Go directly to chemical dependence row.

101
The Group Challenge

Stage: 1-3
Challenge:
   MODERATE
Grades: ALL

GOALS: ▶

- Encourage positive behavior
- Give the group a goal to work towards
- Provide a reward for positive behavior

DESCRIPTION: ▶

Students create a group challenge and a reward for their group to work towards.

DIRECTIONS: ▶

Ask the group to think of something that they could do as a group that wouldn't involve alcohol or other drugs, would be enjoyable to all, and is feasible. For example, they may wish to go roller-skating, have a barbecue in the park, go to a movie, or go on a day hike out in the woods. It's important this activity be one everyone finds enjoyable.

Before they begin planning the specifics for this activity, clarify what the challenge for the group will be. As long as the challenge is focused on personal growth related to chemical dependence issues—continuous abstinence for the support group's duration or improvement in school grades and attendance, for example—encourage the group to decide the specifics of the challenge. It's important that the challenge be specific so that it'll be clear to everyone whether the group met the challenge or not. In order to encourage positive peer pressure, everyone must meet the challenge. If the challenge is perfect school attendance for the duration of the support group, for example, then if one member skips one day, the *entire* group fails the challenge.

It can be helpful to write the challenge in a contract form that everyone signs (see following page for an example). Set aside several minutes of each subsequent group session to monitor the contract. One simple way to do this is to go around the circle and ask everyone if they "made" the contract the past week.

Sometime during the final sessions of group, the specifics of the activity should be planned, such as when and where the activity will take place, rides, and parent permission. Encourage group members to do as much of this as possible.

NOTES:

Before beginning this activity, get the go-ahead from the school administration. It would be tragic if the students followed the contract only to discover that the school won't allow the reward. By the way, the group leaders should also sign the contract, pledging their contributions to the activity.

MATERIALS:

Group Contract.

Group Contract

Our group goal: Everyone in our group will abstain from all mind-altering chemicals for the duration of our support group, which is from January 14th until March 11th. The only chemicals excluded from this list are nicotine, caffeine, alcohol as part of a church service, and chemicals prescribed by a doctor.

Our group reward: If everyone achieves the group goal, we will all go skiing at Echo Valley after the group is over.

Signed   Date

_____   _____

_____   _____

_____   _____

_____   _____

_____   _____

_____   _____

_____   _____

_____   _____

_____   _____

Appendix A: Feelings List

afraid	eager	joyful	scared
aggressive	enraged	lonely	secure
alarmed	enthusiastic	loved	shocked
amused	envious	mad	surprised
angry	exasperated	miserable	tense
annoyed	excited	needed	terrified
anxious	frightened	nervous	threatened
appreciated	frustrated	paranoid	thrilled
bitter	furious	perplexed	troubled
bored	glad	powerful	uneasy
calm	guilty	powerless	unimportant
cautious	happy	puzzled	unloved
comfortable	helpless	regretful	unneeded
concerned	horrified	rejected	unsure
confident	hostile	relieved	wanted
confused	hurt	resentful	worried
contented	inadequate	respected	worthless
crushed	insecure	sad	worthwhile
disappointed	irritated	safe	
discouraged	jealous	satisfied	

The Twelve Steps

1. We admitted we were powerless over alcohol—that our lives had become unmanageable.

2. Came to believe that a Power greater than ourselves could restore us to sanity.

3. Made a decision to turn our will and our lives over to the care of God as we understood Him.

4. Made a searching and fearless moral inventory of ourselves.

5. Admitted to God, to ourselves, and to another human being the exact nature of our wrongs.

6. We were entirely ready to have God remove all these defects of character.

7. Humbly asked Him to remove our shortcomings.

8. Made a list of all persons we had harmed, and became willing to make amends to them all.

9. Made direct amends to such people whenever possible, except when to do so would injure them or others.

10. Continued to take personal inventory and when we were wrong promptly admitted it.

11. Sought through prayer and meditation to improve our conscious contact with God as we understood Him, praying only for knowledge of His will for us and the power to carry that out.

12. Having had a spiritual awakening as a result of these steps, we tried to carry this message to alcoholics, and to practice these principles in all our affairs.

The Twelve Steps are reprinted with permission of Alcoholics Anonymous World Services, Inc. Permission to reprint the Steps does not mean that A.A. has reviewed or approved the contents of this book. A.A. is a program of recovery from alcoholism. Use of the Steps in connection with programs which are patterned after A.A., but which address other problems, does not imply otherwise.

Appendix B: Resources

NOTE: ▶ The following publications are available from Hazelden. Because Hazelden's address and phone numbers are given later in this section, we haven't repeated formal bibliographical data for every item below. If it's not from Hazelden, the name and address is included.

BOOKS: ▶ Anderson, Gary L. *When Chemicals Come to School: The Student Assistance Model.*

Fleming, Martin. *Conducting Support Groups for Students Affected by Chemical Dependence: A Guide for Educators and Other Professionals.*

Fleming, Martin. *101 Support Group Activities for Teenagers Affected by Someone Else's Alcohol/Drug Use.*

Fleming, Martin. *101 Support Group Activities for Teenagers Recovering from Chemical Dependence.*

Freeman, Shelley MacKay. *From Peer Pressure to Peer Support: Alcohol/Drug Prevention Through Group Process—A Curriculum for Grades 7-12.*

Jesse, Rosalie Cruise. *Children in Recovery.*

Johnson, Vernon. *Intervention: How to Help Someone Who Doesn't Want Help.*

Leite, Evelyn, and Pamela Espeland. *Different Like Me: A Book for Teens Who Worry About Their Parents' Use of Alcohol/Drugs.*

Schaefer, Dick. *Choices and Consequences: What to Do When a Teenager Uses Alcohol/Drugs.*

Schmidt, Teresa, and Thelma Spencer. *Building Trust, Making Friends: Tanya Talks About Chemical Dependence in the Family.*

Wilmes, David. *Parenting for Prevention: How to Raise a Child to Say No to Alcohol/Drugs—for Parents, Teachers, and Other Concerned Adults.*

BOOKLETS: ▶ Cloninger, Robert. *Genetic and Environmental Factors Leading to Alcoholism.*

Leite, Evelyn. *Detachment: The Art of Letting Go While Living with an Alcoholic.*

Leite, Evelyn. *How It Feels To Be Chemically Dependent.*

WORKBOOKS: ▶ Fleming, Martin. *How to Stay Clean and Sober: A Relapse Prevention Guide for Teenagers.*

Zarek, David, and James Sipe. *Can I Handle Alcohol/Drugs?*

PERIODICALS: ▶ *Focus on the Family and Chemical Dependence.* 2119-A Hollywood Blvd., Hollywood, FL 33020.

Student Assistance Journal. 1863 Technology Drive, Troy, MI 48083.

VIDEOS: ▶

All the Kids Do It. Pyramid, 1537 14th Street, Box 1048, Santa Monica, CA 90406.

Choices and Consequences. Color, 33 minutes.

Different Like Me: For Teenage Children of Alcoholics. Color, 31 minutes.

The Invisible Line. Color, 30 minutes. Gerald T. Rogers Productions, 5225 Old Orchard Road, Suite 23A, Skokie, IL 60077.

Lots of Kids Like Us. Color, 28 minutes. Gerald T. Rogers Productions, 5225 Old Orchard Road, Suite 23A, Skokie, IL 60077.

My Father's Son: The Legacy of Alcoholism. Color, 33 minutes. Gerald T. Rogers Productions, 5225 Old Orchard Road, Suite 23A, Skokie, IL 60077.

Soft Is the Heart of A Child. Color, 30 minutes.

A Story about Feelings. Color, 10 minutes.

Tell Someone: A Music Video. Color, 4 minutes. Addiction Counselors Continuing Education Services, P.O. Box 30380, Indianapolis, IN 46230.

Where's Shelley? Color, 13 minutes.

Wasted: A True Story. Color, 28 minutes. MTI Teleprograms, Inc., 3710 Commercial Avenue, Northbrook, IL 60062.

OTHER RESOURCES: ▶

Black, Claudia. *The Stamp Game.* MAC Publishing, 5005 E. 39th Avenue, Denver, CO 80207, (303) 331-0148.

ASSESSMENT INSTRUMENTS: ▶

Mayer, J. and Filstead, W. J. *The Adolescent Alcohol Involvement Scale: An Instrument for Measuring Adolescents' Use and Misuse of Alcohol. Journal of Studies on Alcohol,* 1979, 40, 291-300.

Personal Experience Screening Questionnaire (PESQ) by Ken Winters. Western Psychological Services, 12031 Wilshire Blvd., Los Angeles, CA 90025-1251, (800) 648-8857.

Substance Abuse Subtle Screening Inventory (SASSI) by Glenn Miller. The SASSI Institute, 4403 Trailridge Road. Bloomington, IN 47408, (800) 726-0526.

NATIONAL ORGANIZATIONS: ▶

Children of Alcoholics Foundation, Inc. (COAF)
P.O. Box 4185
Grand Central Station
New York, NY 10163
(212) 754-0656

Hazelden
15251 Pleasant Valley Road
Center City, MN 55012
(651) 213-4000 or (800) 328-9000
http://www.hazelden.org

National Association for Children of Alcoholics (NACoA)
11426 Rockville Pike, Suite 100
Rockville, MD 20852
(301) 468-0985

National Council on Alcoholism and Drug Dependence (NCADD)
12 West 21st Street
New York, NY 10010
(212) 206-6770